Blessing Encounters

Blessing Encounters

Creating Family One Blessing at a Time

By

James M. Burns, Jr.
and
Paul M. Burns

Copyright © 2014 by James M. Burns, Jr. and Paul M. Burns
All rights reserved.
ISBN-10: 1499708092
ISBN-13: 978-1499708097

Some of the names in this book have been changed to protect the privacy of those involved.

Unless otherwise noted, the Scripture quotations contained herein are from the New Revised Standard Version Bible, copyright 1989, by the Division of Christian Education of the National Council of the Churches of Christ in the U.S.A. Used by permission. All rights reserved.

Other Scripture quotations come from the English Standard Version, the King James Version, *The Message*, and The New International Version.

Scripture quotations marked (ESV) are from The Holy Bible, English Standard Version® (ESV®), copyright © 2001 by Crossway, a publishing ministry of Good News Publishers. Used by permission. All rights reserved.

Scripture taken from *The Message*. Copyright © 1993, 1994, 1995, 1996, 2000, 2001, 2002. Used by permission of NavPress Publishing Group.

THE HOLY BIBLE, NEW INTERNATIONAL VERSION®, NIV® Copyright © 1973, 1978, 1984, 2011 by Biblica, Inc.® Used by permission. All rights reserved worldwide.

Contents

	Preface	ix
1	Family	1
2	Will	7
3	Blessing	13
4	Belonging	19
5	Strife	25
6	An Ever-Widening Family	33
7	Jesus	39
8	Chuy	45
9	Siri	51
10	Sunday Dinner	57
11	Love	63
12	Welcoming	67
13	Church	73
14	Budapest	79
15	Salvation	87
16	Adoption	95

17	Death	103
18	Resurrection	111
	Epilogue	119
	Notes	123
	Acknowledgements	125
	About the Authors	129

Preface

Paul says . . .

I remember what it was like to be on a New York City subway line stuffed with humanity from all over the world and yet to somehow feel alone. Each person seemed to be living in his or her own solitary bubble. Ears shut closed off with headphones. Eyes focused on a newspaper or a book. Mouths opened only for the occasional muffled cough. Bodies presented as fortresses of solitude not to be disturbed.

Then something happened to the city that would change everything: 9/11.

I remember the first day I went back to work shortly after the horror of that day. I stepped into the elevator of my high-rise apartment building, and there was the fiancé of a young man who had worked on the eighty-eighth floor of one of the towers. His entire company had been lost. The last time I had seen this young woman had been at their engagement party two weeks earlier. I barely recognized her now. She was incapable of recognizing me. I did not say a word. I stayed in my bubble and left her to hers.

As we walked out onto East Ninety-Sixth Street, something was different. No honking horns, just the whir of vehicles and squealing of bus brakes. We stepped together into the same subway train. It was dead quiet. People seemed to be aware that in each of the bubbles of existence present around them there might be incredible pain. The silence was respect.

Over the next few days the silence began to be replaced by soft conversations between strangers. They all revolved around the shared experience of the day of the terrorist attack. Where were you? Did you lose anyone? What did you see or hear? One by one, bubbles began to pop. Lives poured out and mingled with other lives.

One word I heard a lot was *bless*. God bless. God bless this nation. God bless this city. God bless your family. Suddenly this secular city had become a place of blessing. People were encountering each other on trains and buses, in bars, and even, some, in churches. In fact, church attendance skyrocketed for a period. Some found God there, and many found each other. This is something. I believe God can be found when we deeply encounter one another. I believe God blesses us in and through these encounters. I believe, even more amazingly, God creates family out of such encounters. We gain brothers, sisters, fathers, daughters, grandparents.

I never spoke to that young woman. I will never know the depth of pain she was experiencing that day. Perhaps there was nothing I could have said, but I wish I had reached out beyond my bubble and blessed her in some way so that she might know she was not alone in this world.

Blessing Encounters is a testament to the value of recognizing our shared existence on this planet and our shared relationship through our common Creator. Within its pages is a challenge to us to pop our bubbles of self-isolation and alienation so that we might be a blessing to others and be blessed ourselves. This book has been written in the hope that God will make a family out of our fractured existence, one blessing encounter at a time.

I shared the experience of writing this book with my dad, who, like myself, is a pastor. After all, how can a person write a book about family all by himself? God didn't. God used a whole team of writers, and they were all family. God's family.

Peace,
Rev. Paul M. Burns
Priest Lake Presbyterian Church
Nashville, Tennessee

Jim says . . .

You never know when you will be blessed.

> It happened to me one day when our son Paul called me and said, "Dad, I want you to write a book with me."

> Paul is persistent. That is one of his strengths as a pastor.

> So I knew we would be writing this book.

Both of us believe life is filled with blessing encounters. Blessings that occur as people choose to engage with, instead of avoid, one another.

> Next to God, the greatest blessing of my life resulted from a conversation with a friend.

> He said, "Jim, when are you going to ask Judy Clements out?"

> I was trying to finish graduate school. I had no time for a new relationship.

>> But I called up this girl I had met one weekend at a Christian retreat and asked her to go to a movie with me.

>> And I never quit calling. Four months later we were engaged. By the time you read this, we will have celebrated at least forty-five years of blessing encounters.

Now do not get me wrong. Not every day of marriage has been a blessing encounter.

> We human beings have the power to bless, but we also have the power to curse. Living with others is a mixture of blessings and curses.

>> The trick is to figure out how to tilt the balance to blessing.

For me it begins with remembering the words in an old hymn, "Morning by morning new mercies I see," and then thanking God for both the new mercies and the old.

Seeing and thanking. And doing. Doing what I can to bless others. That is the way I go about opening my life to blessing encounters.

As we bring good into the lives of other people, we create community.

We help bring families of blessing into existence. Families that include our closest loved ones and families that include friends and even some who may be enemies.

Wherever two or more people gather and bless one another, there is a family.

You can be in a bowling league and discover you have been blessed by your team having become another family for you.

You can sit next to a stranger on a plane, listen to that person, open yourself up in return, maybe even pray for your seatmate, and a family has been created. Even if you never see that person again.

Paul's first book is titled *Prayer Encounters: Changing the World One Prayer at a Time.*

I love that book. What a blessing it has been to many people!

Prayer is one way in which people bless one another. But blessing encounters occur in many other ways as well.

We speak words of encouragement, we offer deeds of caring, we forgive and are forgiven, we sit with those who are sick, we listen to a teenager whose body is spinning in a hundred different ways, we toss a ball to a child who tosses it back—

there is no end to the ways in which we bless and are blessed when we connect with others.

This book can be read alone, but it is best heard with others.

Each chapter can be read in the first five or ten minutes after your group has gathered. The three questions at the end of each chapter will facilitate a discussion that will probably raise new questions.

At the end of every chapter is a challenge designed to help everyone in your group create blessings among the people they encounter in their lives. Close with the prayer, and go forth to create family and change the world.

One blessing at a time.

Grace and Blessings,
Rev. James M. Burns, Jr.
Retired, but still trying to
create blessing encounters
Norman, Oklahoma

Chapter 1

Family

Then God said, "Let us make humankind in our image, according to our likeness; and let them have dominion over the fish of the sea, and over the birds of the air, and over the cattle, and over all the wild animals of the earth, and over every creeping thing that creeps upon the earth."

So God created humankind in his
    image,
  in the image of God he created
    them;
  male and female he created them.

God blessed them, and God said to them, "Be fruitful and multiply, and fill the earth and subdue it; and have dominion over the fish of the sea and over the birds of the air and over every living thing that moves upon the earth."

    — Genesis 1:26–28

Then the LORD God formed man from the dust of the ground, and breathed into his nostrils the breath of life; and the man became a living being. . . .

The LORD God took the man and put him in the garden of Eden to till it and keep it. And the LORD God commanded the man, "You may freely eat of every tree of the garden; but of the tree of the knowledge of good and evil you shall not eat, for in the day that you eat of it you shall die.

Then the LORD God said, "It is not good that the man should be alone; I will make him a helper as his partner."

— Genesis 2:7, 15–18

Jim says . . .

It was Christmas Eve 1948.

I stood in my grandparents' living room, a few feet from the Christmas tree.

Two days earlier I had celebrated my fifth birthday. Now, at my parents' invitation, I stood up and began reciting from memory, "'Twas the night before Christmas . . ." all the way to the end of that favorite childhood poem.

Throughout the first two decades and more of my life I spent every Christmas Eve at my grandparents' house in Goliad, Texas.

In the afternoon my father, mother, sister, and I would travel the thirty miles from our home in Beeville to Goliad.

It might have been an entire year since my sister and I had last seen our two cousins, but we would begin playing as if we had been together only the day before.

As dinnertime neared, we would walk a few blocks to my great-aunt's home. "Nannie," we called her.

Soon we were eating ham, peas, ambrosia, coleslaw, and more.

Then back to my grandparents' home to open Christmas gifts.

My grandmother always bought a tree so small that the

> presents piled halfway up its height.
>
> We cousins would be the designated elves. We would pass out the presents to our family, never questioning the fact that we would not open our own until we had finished our assigned task.

As I gave my recitation on that Christmas Eve of 1948, those gathered around me included my parents, my aunts and uncles, cousins, grandparents, grandmother's sisters, and the great-grandfather who had been born while Abraham Lincoln was president.

We read in Genesis chapter 2, "It is not good that the man should be alone" (v. 18).

> On those Christmas Eves in Goliad, I never felt alone. I felt surrounded by people who knew me, who praised me, who loved me.
>
> I was in the midst of family.

Author Jim Butcher famously said, "When everything goes to hell, the people who stand by you without flinching—they are your family."

> I am certain my parents flinched more times than I can ever imagine, but they always stood by me.
>
> What I did not know when I was young is that some people never have that experience. I was very fortunate.

As years passed, the theme of family was always on my mind and heart. I began to realize the concept of family is much bigger than I knew at age five.

ಐ ಆ

One day, years ago, I called a parishioner, and his four-year-old daughter, Rachel, answered the phone.

> She was polite. Poised. She knew her business.
>
> After exchanging opening pleasantries, I told Rachel I was calling to speak to her father.
>
>> "Who are you?" she wanted to know.
>>
>> "I'm Jim Burns."
>>
>> Pause.
>>
>> Then Rachel tossed back, "You go to *my* church."

Thinking back to those words, I realize what had already happened to Rachel at age four is what a pastor yearns for every person who attends a church to experience.

> She had been incorporated into the body. She had a stake in what went on there and ownership in this community of Presbyterian Jesus people.
>
> She lived in the midst of family. A family that extended way beyond her parents and siblings, and grandparents, and aunts, and uncles, and cousins.
>
> Rachel was not alone. She belonged.

As for me, I was always very pleased to attend Rachel's church.

ೞ ଓ

It is not good for us to be alone. What is good is for us to join with others in saying and living good news to God's world.

What is good is for me to recognize that my family, like Rachel's, goes way beyond those people who surrounded me on Christmas Eve 1948.

What is good is for me to keep learning how to open my mind, my heart, my soul, and my arms to all the brothers and sisters God has given us on this planet.

Paul says . . .

The word *family* comes from the Latin *familia,* which encompasses the servants of a household as well as the blood relations. Even as late as the fifteenth century, in English *family* was understood as being all those dwelling under the same roof, including the servants and boarders, "under one head." It was not until the seventeenth century that the meaning was narrowed to encompass just parents and their children regardless of their geographical proximity to one another. In some ways this limits the definition of what a family is; but in another way it expands it greatly, making relationship more important than physical nearness.

Ah, but we need both definitions.

When my family goes out to eat, my young son, Nelson, always gravitates toward children his age. He is fascinated with the other little ones nearby. He relates. They speak his language, whatever that is. When he spots that other child who is like him, it is as if he is saying, "At last! Bone of my bones! Flesh of my flesh! Here is one like me!" Just as when the man first saw the woman. It was not their differences he was so struck by, it was their similarities. She was one who was like him! She was one to whom he could relate. "Bone of my bones and flesh of my flesh" (Gen. 2:23). A relative. Family.

Questions

1. In what situations did you feel most not alone as you were growing up?

2. What families (beyond your blood family) do you belong to at present?

3. What are specific projects you have joined with others in doing? As you worked with them on those projects, did you feel you became a family? Why or why not?

Family Challenge

Think of one person in your life, someone who may or may not be a blood family member, who is more alone than most. Find ways to invite that person more deeply into your family circle.

Prayer

God our Creator, we thank you for choosing to place us in families. And we thank you for the opportunity to create new families while we were becoming adults. Give us wisdom and grace to welcome into our family circles people who may not live life on the same page as we do. Give us insight and energy to work together doing whatever you call us to do. In the Spirit of Christ we pray. Amen.

Chapter 2

Will

While he was still speaking to the people, behold, his mother and his brothers stood outside, asking to speak to him. But he replied to the man who told him, "Who is my mother, and who are my brothers?" And stretching out his hand toward his disciples, he said, "Here are my mother and my brothers! For whoever does the will of my Father in heaven is my brother and sister and mother."

— Matthew 12:46–50, English Standard Version

Paul says . . .

I have observed many people fighting cancer. It is a difficult thing to experience, and it is at such a time that people lean most heavily on their family. But what if you do not have a family?

Jo is such a person. Most of her family has passed away, and what blood relations she does have are distant. She and her husband, Mike, have gone through much of their life without kin. Although they have both struggled with a variety of disabilities, somehow they always manage to roll along in life, finding people along the way to help them. When Jo was diagnosed with stage 3 breast cancer, I wondered who would be there for her. Mike, whose dementia was increasing, had recently been placed in a nursing facility.

On the morning of Jo's double mastectomy, I battled my way through rush hour traffic to the hospital with a big, thick book at my side to keep me company in the waiting room. I arrived at the nurses' station to ask for her room number and found a woman standing in front of me, beating me to the punch. After exchanging surprised introductions, we went together to the tiny room in which Jo had been prepped for surgery.

Jo was so happy to see us. "I see you've met each other," she beamed, as pleased as a mother witnessing the reunion of estranged children. Martha and I smiled and nodded.

Before we could even take a seat, the door opened, and a petite woman burst into the room. "I made it! Traffic was horrible!" This was Kim. She looked at Martha and me, not surprised at all to see a growing collection of supporters in the room. Jo introduced us to each other with great joy and pride. It was quite a full house.

We chatted for a while, and then Jo asked if I would share some scripture. While we were discussing the passage I had read, a tech came in to take Jo off to surgery. But first we all joined hands, including the tech, Thomas, with whom Jo was already on a first-name basis, and we prayed.

Then Thomas took her away, and we all adjourned to the waiting room. There we began to share how each of us knew Jo. Martha was a nurse assistant at the retirement building where Jo lives. Jo had befriended her and been a great spiritual support to her. They had become true spiritual sisters.

Kim had known Jo since 1992. She did Jo's nails. At the time they met, Kim was not a person of faith. She attributes her faith to Jo's loving nurture over the years. She shared her own profound story of salvation and forgiveness.

After we had been talking nonstop for a few hours, Maggie, an elder from my church, showed up. Maggie, who has a real estate license, had helped Jo and Mike when their house had gone into foreclosure, before Maggie was even a member of the church.

We all shared our Jo stories. Some were funny, others deeply moving. My big, thick book sat untouched by my side. What a life this woman had had!

And what a family she had that day. A God-made family.

No one should go through life alone. We need family, and we need to be family. Jesus—who did not define his own family on the basis of biology, gender, race, nationality, or cultural tradition—constantly pulls us and pushes us into a larger conception of family. He will not stop either, not until we recognize ourselves, along with all humanity, as being one family with God.

Being family for others requires an intentional will to do so. This is the will of God.

Jim says . . .

Rarely do I find myself walking in lockstep with my sisters and brothers in Christ.

We may all agree that we are called to love our neighbors; but the question is, how do we go about putting our love into action?

And many of us will have a different answer to that question.

Furthermore, another person may be better equipped than we with the necessary skills and innate traits to offer the love and help a neighbor may need.

I have a friend who has been a very good counselor to his teenage niece because he has been through some of what she is currently facing.

Although I know his niece well and can support her in other ways, my friend can hear her in a way I cannot, and he can offer advice I have little qualification to give.

That does not, however, mean I have nothing to offer.

I can pray, and I can find other ways to lend support.

As the apostle Paul teaches us in Corinthians, we are each a part of Christ's body, but we are different parts (1 Cor. 12:12–31).

Together we become a family that says yes to Christ as we carry out the "will of [our] Father in heaven" (Matt. 12:50).

Questions

1. How is Jesus' conception of what a family is similar or different from your own?

2. Have you ever gone through a struggle in which you felt alone?

3. How have you been family to another person to whom you are not related?

Family Challenge

The next time you hear of someone in your neighborhood, workplace, church, or some other social circle who is struggling, be family for that person. Call or visit as if that person is your own mother, father, brother, sister, or child.

Prayer

May the Father of us all open our hearts to have the will to be family for others in their time of need. In the name of our older brother, Jesus. Amen.

Chapter 3

Blessing

Now the LORD said to Abram, "Go from your country and your kindred and your father's house to the land that I will show you. I will make of you a great nation, and I will bless you, and make your name great, so that you will be a blessing. I will bless those who bless you, and the one who curses you I will curse; and in you all the families of the earth shall be blessed."

So Abram went, as the LORD had told him; and Lot went with him. Abram was seventy-five years old when he departed from Haran.

— Genesis 12:1–4

By contrast, the fruit of the Spirit is love, joy, peace, patience, kindness, generosity, faithfulness, gentleness, and self-control. There is no law against such things.

— Galatians 5:22-23

Jim says . . .

A friend was teaching a Bible class for children in a Sunday school classroom that was unfamiliar to him. On the walls were various posters, some with Bible verses.

At one point he asked the class how they had been blessed. One little girl answered, "By the fruit of the Spirit."

"Do you know what the fruit of the Spirit is?" my friend queried.

> The girl quickly answered, "Love, joy, peace . . ." and rattled off the entire list.

Surprised, he asked, "How did you know that?"

> She replied matter-of-factly, "They're listed on the wall right behind you."

That is how it is with blessings. Sometime the blessing is right behind us. Or maybe even right in front of us, and we do not see it.

In Psalm 23 we hear, "Surely goodness and mercy shall follow me all the days of my life" (v. 6).

> All the days. Even the dark days. If I just look behind me, the blessings of goodness and mercy are always there.

☼ ☙

The word *blessing* first appears in the Bible in Genesis 12 when God said to Abram,

> "I will bless you, and make your name great, so that you will be a blessing. . . . in you all the families of the earth shall be blessed" (vv. 2, 3).

Although I am not a descendant of Abram—or Abraham, as he came to be called—I am blessed because of him.

> That is the plan. One person is blessed, and through him others are blessed.
>
> We receive God's blessing, which usually comes through other people, and we go out and create families by blessing the people in our lives.

One blessing at a time. This is how a family is created. Or, rather, this is how a blessed family is created.

> My wife and I are called to bless our children and to bless each other. In doing so, we get closer to God's picture of what a family is supposed to be.
>
> But this goes beyond our kinfolks. It includes our church. It includes the riotous bunco group my wife gathers with every month. It includes the small group of retired ministers I sip coffee and munch cookies with on the back porch of an aging yet energetic Episcopal priest. For some it includes their fellow members of the board of a wealthy corporation. For others it includes all those who work for a struggling nonprofit agency. Family encompasses every grouping of human beings imaginable.
>
> Never are we just a group gathered to do business. Always, we are creating invisible bonds with one another, with the result being that we become family. And as with most families, we are either blessing one another or cursing one another, and sometimes both.

ஐ ௸

Like Johnny Appleseed of old, we are called to sprinkle blessings wherever we go.

To me this means we sprinkle good no matter where we are. Good that comes in many forms. Through a deed, through a word. Sometimes I pray a prayer asking God to surround people with God's love, care, presence, and protection.

The Reverend Tice has said "a blessing from G-d is empowerment to be able to do what is not within our natural capabilities." If this is so, then I believe we are agents of God who are called to pass on blessings that help people be and do more than they thought they could be and do.

As we sprinkle blessings, we help make the groups, or families, in which we live stronger. We marvel as we see love, joy, peace, patience, goodness, and all the rest of the fruit of the Spirit blossom and flourish (Gal. 5:22–23).

ಬ ಡ

I am reminded of a time the children's choir was singing at our church. Someone told one of the children how much his singing was appreciated.

> The child responded, "I was singing for God." He then went on to say, "But the thing about God is that he never shows up."

I hope this was a passing phase in this child's life. I hope he has known many times since then when God has indeed shown up. I hope he has come to realize one of the main ways God shows up is through the people of God in whom the love, care, presence, and protection of Christ lives.

Creating family one blessing at a time. The blessing I would give to this child would be:

> God really does show up. Keep hanging with God's people. Keep your eyes and ears and mind and heart alert. Keep singing for

God.

May we all keep singing for God, and by the singing of our lives may we help build links that create a world of diverse families who do more than we can think or imagine.

Paul says . . .

I met the man I now call my best friend on the veranda outside the lunchroom of the seminary at which we had both just arrived as new students, and we quickly became engrossed in the first of a thousand theological discussions. By the end of that first one, I began to sense that in speaking with this fellow I was becoming more me. Over many years of friendship we have both come to understand that there is no Michael without Paul, and no Paul without Michael. It is as if God crafted a piece of me and placed it in Michael so that through my relationship with him I might become more fully me.

I believe that God places pieces of ourselves in other people. If this is indeed the case, then you and I will never be completed until we have not only met all of the people who contain our puzzle pieces but also allowed each of them to bless us with that piece through a relationship with them.

We must seek others and hold them tight and occasionally wrestle with them, as Jacob wrestled with the angel in Genesis 32:22–32, to receive their blessing, that missing puzzle piece of our identity. Honestly, some relationships are a bit like a wrestling match, but there is blessing in the wrestling.

As we wrestle in faith with God and others, there is no end to the fruit that will be harvested.

Questions

1. How have you been blessed in the last week?

2. How have you blessed others in the last week?

3. Why could it be said that even the board of a wealthy corporation is a family? In what ways can this group become a family that is richly blessed?

Family Challenge

Keep a daily journal over the next seven days. Record each blessing you see in which you have been blessed by your family or a group in which you are a member. Record each blessing you give to your family or a group in which you are a member.

Prayer

God of blessing, we thank you for the goodness and mercy that always follow us. We thank you for the "love, joy, peace, patience, kindness, generosity, faithfulness, gentleness, and self-control" that others have showered on our lives (Gal. 5:22–23). May we be a blessing to each group in which we live our lives so that we empower other people to look and live more like Christ each day. Amen

Chapter 4

Belonging

For just as each of us has one body with many members, and these members do not all have the same function, so in Christ we, though many, form one body, and each member belongs to all the others.

— Romans 12:4–5, New International Version

Paul says . . .

One of my favorite times of the week is Wednesday evenings with my church's high school youth program. At the end of our devotional time we gather in a circle at the front of the sanctuary and hold hands. Taking turns, we share any answered prayers we have experienced since we met last.

Since beginning this practice, I have seen an enormous difference in both the way the youth pray and what they pray for. Before, the other leaders and I could barely get them to pray for anything. Once they began to experience answered prayer, though, they began to pray more frequently and more fervently.

We always pray for more youth to join us. This is one of my favorite prayer requests because when it happens, we can truthfully tell the new youths with us that they are an answer to our prayers. They always beam. I love it.

Our high schoolers are a mix of children raised in the church and children from the neighborhood who come to us primarily through our Summer Hoops basketball program. Every year a few new neighborhood kids from the basketball program join our youth program. It always takes some time for a new teen who has never been part of a church or a youth group to learn how to behave in this kind of gathering. Sometimes this poses a great challenge to both the leaders and the other youth.

One of the new kids who recently joined has been particularly challenging. La'Shawn was invited by Devon, another boy whose behavior has been equally challenging. At one point we had to suspend both of them from coming for two weeks. One of them shouted indignantly, "You can't kick us out! This is church!"

"Exactly," I replied, hearing my father's voice in my own. "Church is where we respect and love each other, and you are doing neither. I want you to think hard about why you come here."

We were not sure if we would see them again. But after two weeks, there they were, ready for more. I am not saying they were angels after that, but we have seen improvement. Baby steps.

After we finished our devotion and began to circle up for prayer the night they returned to us, our two trouble boys practically wrestled each other to get to the spot on my left to hold my hand in the prayer circle. La'Shawn won. He took my hand, and we all began to pray. I felt love and respect from both of those boys, if only for a few moments.

I am not sure either La'Shawn or Devon can articulate why they come to youth night every week. It is perhaps too deep for words. I think they want to belong.

༄ ༅

There is no deeper human desire than to belong.

I remember loving going to summer church camp. I felt as if there I could be exactly who I was. It was an amazing feeling of freedom and of being loved no matter what. I felt as if I belonged, something I had never really felt at school. Eventually, I allowed the identity nurtured at camp to become my identity all year, like it or lump it. I knew that I belonged somewhere.

Perhaps there is no worse feeling than realizing you do not belong. That sense of alienation is the great human pain. It is the feeling you get when you know you have to hide yourself so that you will be accepted on some level. It is the deep-down sorrow of not fitting in. Perhaps it was the feeling Adam had before there was Eve, when it was just him and the animals. What an amazing feeling must have come over Adam as he declared, "This at last is bone of my bones and flesh of my flesh" (Gen. 2:23).

Through Christ we belong to God. We become part of the family. We are made bone of his bones and flesh of his flesh by

God's grace as we believe it and accept it. We are accepted, and our true identity begins to emerge.

The apostle Paul wrote in his letter to the Romans that each member of the body of Christ belongs to all the other members (12:5). That belonging is something we practice in our churches. It can be practiced in many other ways as well. We can offer belonging to our neighbors near and far. We can help people know they belong. We can meet people in the pain of their alienation and invite them to belong with us.

Jim says . . .

"God is good. All the time."

> This simple statement quickly brings back memories.
>
> I was with a group of young people on a church ski trip. The theme of our week, which we addressed every evening in our Bible study gathering, was "Praying the Slopes." We each had a prayer partner we were to remember throughout that week.
>
>> We found ourselves crying out "God is good!" to each other whenever we saw one of our group on the snow or up on a chair lift, and we would hear the joyful response, "All the time!"
>
> In those few days our community deepened from what we had experienced back home in the Sunday night youth group.
>
>> We belonged to one another.
>>
>> We were brothers and sisters in Christ.
>>
>> We were family.
>
> This deeper, Christ-like belonging does not just happen.

It occurs when there is a true "be-longing," as we find ourselves *longing* to *be* with people, to know their joys and sufferings, to work together with them to create a better world, to build a pocket of peace here and a corner of love there.

It is odd to me how biological families can maintain such a strong bond even when their members say and do terrible things to one another.

A person may not travel two hundred miles to attend the funeral of a good friend, while a family member may go halfway across the country to attend a disliked family member's funeral.

The promise of Christ is that a day is coming when we will experience that close, close bond with all sisters and brothers, and it will be strengthened because we say and do only that which helps the other.

God is indeed good. All the time.

And the times are going to get even "gooder."

Questions

1. Have you ever felt as if you did not belong, were out of place? When and why?

2. What groups and people do you belong to?

3. How can you help others feel as if they belong?

Family Challenge

Include someone new in your circle this week, whether it be in your neighborhood or at work, play, or church.

Prayer

O Lord, in whom we find our deepest ground of belonging, you have included us in your holy family. Help me to include others in my circle. In your circle of love—Father, Son, and Holy Spirit. Amen.

Chapter 5

Strife

Now the man knew his wife Eve, and she conceived and bore Cain, saying, "I have produced a man with the help of the LORD." Next she bore his brother Abel. Now Abel was a keeper of sheep, and Cain a tiller of the ground. In the course of time Cain brought to the LORD an offering of the fruit of the ground, and Abel for his part brought of the firstlings of his flock, their fat portions. And the Lord had regard for Abel and his offering, but for Cain and his offering he had no regard. So Cain was very angry, and his countenance fell. The Lord said to Cain, 'Why are you angry, and why has your countenance fallen? If you do well, will you not be accepted? And if you do not do well, sin is lurking at the door; its desire is for you, but you must master it.'

Cain said to his brother Abel, 'Let us go out to the field.' And when they were in the field, Cain rose up against his brother Abel and killed him.

— Genesis 4:1–8

Those conflicts and disputes among you, where do they come from? Do they not come from your cravings that are at war within you? You want something and do not have it; so you commit murder. And you covet something and cannot obtain it; so you engage in disputes and conflicts. You do not have, because you do not ask. You ask and do not receive, because you ask wrongly, in order to spend what you get on your pleasures.

— James 4:1–3

Jim says . . .

How stupid I was.

It was a muggy summer night, and we were having a youth lock-in. Things had started well but begun to unravel. The four teenage boys in the group were driving me crazy. I had asked them to draw a footprint representing their walk, their journey in life, and to write on the footprint various strengths they saw themselves as having.

The snickering and horseplay increased as I tried to get them to focus on this serious work. The group also included one girl, who quietly and carefully attended to the assignment. But the boys would not settle down.

Sighing with exasperation, I barked, "Follow me," and marched down the hall and out the door of the church with the four mystified boys and one puzzled girl lagging behind.

"Do you see that?" I directed my question specifically to the boys as I stood there in my jean shorts and no shoes.

I pointed to the flower garden nestled next to the church building. A young member of our church had created it for his Eagle Scout project. The garden displayed the Boy Scout's careful planning and ability to carry out a challenging project.

With focused intensity I told them, "That's what responsibility is about. That's what you're missing tonight." Blank stares informed me my words were not having the effect I intended. My agenda for the night had not been their agenda.

I then turned to go back into the church building.

The door was locked. I did not have my key with me. There was no one else in the building to let us in. And now it was midnight. I was not happy. It may be that the boys, and perhaps the girl as well, took some small delight in seeing a grownup in a situation in which he, unlike the Eagle Scout, had not planned carefully enough.

Barefooted, I led the group, whose interest was clearly piqued by the unexpected turn of events, to a gas station a block away. I used the station's phone to call my wife and said, "Please come to the church, and make sure you have your key."

An hour later everyone in the group was safely deposited in their homes. The lock-in was over. I was done. I was defeated.

> I had no interest in continuing what was intended to be an all-night event. I had no more life lessons to teach them that night, as I was vaguely aware that I myself had a few things to learn about working with young people. I wanted to head home, go to sleep, and start over again in the morning.

Twenty years have passed since that night. The four boys are now grown men with jobs. They have found the right partner to spend their lives with. Three of them have children and are excellent fathers. They are good and respectful and productive people.

> And they love and respect me. Because they know, like I know, that you win some and you lose some. Because they know that, angry as I was that night, I cared for them deeply.

One man I know has a son who was a mess in his late teenage years. His mother, in frustration, kicked him out of the house. But now, years later, he is a fine husband and father. He has a good job. He is active in his church.

> His father tried to "fix" him back in those days. The son, however, said the main way his parents helped was by letting him know they were always there for him and by they themselves living the kind of life that leads to health and not disorder.

☙ ❧

The psychologist M. Scott Peck has said one of the purposes of marriage "is for the friction."

> Friction? What in the world do you mean?
>
> In the friction, the strife, that goes on in a marriage, Dr. Peck said, people are challenged to grow. The mere presence of the other changes us.

Perhaps the same is true of any close relationship. We encounter trouble with our friend. Perhaps it leads to rupture, to separation, to an alienation that never finds reconciliation. But often, out of the trouble and strife, a new relationship is born that is even more meaningful. Our bond has been threatened, and we have withstood the threat and grown stronger.

The subtitle of this book is "Creating Family One Blessing at a Time." Perhaps this chapter could be titled "Creating Relationship One War (or Argument) at a Time."

> We pray for a day when wars will cease. But we are thankful God can use our wars, whether between nations or within families, to bless us into becoming the kind of people God wants us to be and we want ourselves to be.

I think now and then of those first brothers, Cain and Abel. I think of what is said in the fourth chapter of James: "You desire but do not have, so you kill" (v. 2, NIV).

I do not know what Abel had that Cain wanted. But I think it was some desire gone awry in Cain that led him to commit the first murder recorded in the Bible.

> Every day people kill one another. Sometimes they kill the body, though often it is a killing of spirit and soul. All because we want

something that really is not ours to have.

☙ ❧

I wanted teenage boys to behave like adults that hot summer night.

> I know better now. I know what my minister friend Mac knew when a number of church youth groups had gathered for a lock-in at his church one night. The kids were being rowdy, but Mac spread out his sleeping bag in the middle of the fellowship hall, lay down, and seemingly went to sleep.
>
> > I watched in amazement. He did nothing. As far as I was concerned, he had abdicated his responsibility. Yet, it was not long before the room settled down and the horseplay stopped.

I know better now, but I am still learning. Not too many wars anymore, but I still engage in skirmishes with people. Admittedly, the skirmishes sometimes make me feel alive, though sometimes I feel stupid and wonder, why in the world did I do what I just did?

What I am certain about is this: God is in the business of creating family, bringing people together.

> Even in strife, God finds ways to bless us.

Paul says . . .

My twin brother, David, and I were not the fighting types when we were growing up. Mainly we enjoyed each other's company and respected each other's stuff. One time, though, in the third grade, out on the playground at recess, I became filled with strife.

I really liked a girl named Jennifer. While she and I were playing some child's game, David joined us. It was not long before it began to occur to me that Jennifer seemed to like David more than she did me. Whether this is true or not I will never know; but in that moment when I pushed my brother as hard as I could from behind, I knew I had done something horrible.

David crumpled to the ground, taken totally unawares. We were both shocked by what I had done. We reconciled immediately, and he was not hurt. I cannot even remember how Jennifer responded, but it did not matter. What mattered was my brother.

We eventually both found our own Jennifers—literally, because David and I both married women named Jennifer—and are married to them to this day. The other Jennifer, the one who came between us, is in the past.

In his letter to the Ephesians, the apostle Paul wrote, "For [Christ] is our peace; in his flesh he has made both groups into one and has broken down the dividing wall, that is, the hostility between us" (2:14). Ever since Cain killed Abel, brothers have been killing each other in some way or another. Christ was sent to remove the strife that keeps us divided. The old hymn declares, "The strife is o'er, the battle done; the victory of life is won; the song of triumph has begun." But not everyone is singing this song yet.

Every so often I awake from a bad dream, and, though I know I am awake, I still find myself trying to get back into the dream to finish the fight. It takes me a few minutes to ask myself, why am I trying to get back to that stupid dream? It's over.

Jesus is awakening us from our strife-filled dreams. But we still find ourselves wanting to climb back into bed with them. The song of triumph has begun, the question is: Will you join in the chorus?

Questions

1. In Ecclesiastes 3 we hear there is "a time for war, and a time for peace" (v. 8). Will we ever enter a time in which war is no longer? If so, how do you think we will get there?

2. In what ways have you been blessed through strife with others?

3. Has anyone ever "killed" you? If so, did resurrection/reconciliation occur in that relationship?

Family Challenge

A suggested experiment: when you find yourself headed toward strife with another person, try saying to that person in some way, by word or deed, "I may be wrong, and I love you."

Prayer

God of constant blessing, our desires lead us to hurt other people. Our wants lead us to hurt ourselves. Sometimes we are living in an intolerable war zone in which we do not even know whom to blame. But we do know where to turn—to you, to your wisdom and light and peace. Grant us the will and strength to create blessing out of strife, no matter who caused what. In the Spirit of the Lord of Peace, we offer this prayer. Amen.

Chapter 6

An Ever-Widening Family

Just then a lawyer stood up to test Jesus. "Teacher," he said, "what must I do to inherit eternal life?" He said to him, "What is written in the law? What do you read there?" He answered, "You shall love the Lord your God with all your heart, and with all your soul, and with all your strength, and with all your mind; and your neighbor as yourself." And he said to him, "You have given the right answer; do this, and you will live."

But wanting to justify himself, he asked Jesus, "And who is my neighbor?" Jesus replied, "A man was going down from Jerusalem to Jericho, and fell into the hands of robbers, who stripped him, beat him, and went away, leaving him half dead. Now by chance a priest was going down that road; and when he saw him, he passed by on the other side. So likewise a Levite, when he came to the place and saw him, passed by on the other side. But a Samaritan while traveling came near him; and when he saw him, he was moved with pity. He went to him and bandaged his wounds, having poured oil and wine on them. Then he put him on his own animal, brought him to an inn, and took care of him. The next day he took out two denarii, gave them to the innkeeper, and said, 'Take care of him; and when I come back, I will repay you whatever more you spend.' Which of these three, do you think, was a neighbor to the man who fell into the hands of the robbers?" He said, "The one who showed him mercy." Jesus said to him, "Go and do likewise."

— Luke 10:25–37

Paul says . . .

La'Shawn, who I introduced in chapter 4, showed up at the Summer Hoops basketball program at my church. It was the first time I had seen him that summer. No one seemed to want him on a team this time, which is a shame because he can really play. So instead he just hung out, talking with whoever would listen. And, of course, he chatted all the way through my half-time message.

As we were eating the meal served after our last game of the day, he asked if I could take him home afterward. His family had moved out of walking distance at the end of the school year. I agreed, but I needed to leave early to get home in time for dinner with extended family who were in town to see our new baby.

"La'Shawn," I said, trying to keep the impatience out of my voice. "Please hurry up and eat. I need to get home to my family."

He got up and tossed his plate of half-eaten food in the trash. "Okay. Let's go."

"I didn't mean you had to throw it away," I protested, but he walked on ahead of me.

As we got into the car, he asked, "Was that your wife holding that baby in the back of the gym when I got here?" Yes, it was.

He was silent for a moment. "I tried to call you, but you didn't answer."

I had noticed he had called, but I had been in the middle of something. He had not left a message. "My mom, she had to have surgery," he told me now, in a rush of words. "She lost a baby. It got stuck in her tubes. I wanted you to come pray with her like we do at church. She okay now." He paused and then said, "I ain't gonna cause trouble on Wednesday nights no more. I'll be good."

My family could wait. "Is she at home now?"

"Yeah. I been takin' care of her."

"We could go pray for her now."

He led me up the stairs, went through the apartment's door, and signaled for me to wait at the doorway. He came back a moment later. "She on the balcony." He led me to her.

La'Shawn's mother had the look of dulled pain and grief I have seen many times. She smiled faintly when she saw me. "Hey, Pastor Paul."

We talked a little about what had happened. La'Shawn stood by her. Then I offered to pray. He took my hand with his right hand and his mother's with his left. I took her other hand, and we prayed.

ಬ ಲ

It is hard to give up our idea of family. I want to separate what I think of as my family from those to whom I do not want to be attached. Like the priest and the Levite, I want to walk past the person in need. I am busy, after all. I have my own family to get to.

I recently heard a story told by a man who lives in New York City. A friend of his was coming to visit. It was her first time in New York, her first time in a large city of any kind. He went to pick her up at one of the seediest places in town, the Port Authority. She had arrived on a bus.

As they were leaving the smelly, scary home of unpleasant public transit, they saw a homeless man sitting with his back against the outer wall of the building. He looked horrible and smelled worse. The woman rushed over to him, knelt down beside him, and cried with all sincerity, "Sir! How did this happen?"

The longtime New Yorker looked down on her as if she had lost her mind. Over time, if you live in a city like that, the homeless can begin to look like trash on the curb. You just walk around them without making eye contact.

After giving the man a substantial bit of cash, the woman rejoined her friend on their way to her lodging. The man begin to wonder who had really lost their mind, his friend for helping a man who had most likely been in a constant state of helplessness for most of his life, or himself for ceasing to care.

There are people in the world we would rather not include in our family circle. But if we want to stand in God's family circle, we will have to join hands with the ever-widening family of God. Many of them have been beaten up by the world and left ignored by the roadside of life. Some of them are right in your neighborhood. You may work or go to church with some of them. You may be one of them.

But you stand with them all when you follow Christ into the world.

Jim says . . .

I have a friend who loves animals, especially cats.

> She always keeps cat food in her purse, just in case her life intersects with that of a hungry kitty.
>
> One day while we were in the car, she saw a small dog running down the street. The next thing I knew, we were out of the car chasing after the dog and looking for its owner.
>
> I do not know if her sympathies extend to horses and cows, or even elephants and zebras; but I do know she also cares about people, though admittedly, cats may well be at the top of her list.

As I think about it now, she is drawn to small children as well. After sitting down for dinner in a restaurant, she is prone to pop up and head for a nearby table to admire a baby or a toddler.

Proud parents soak up the words of praise she showers upon their child.

My wife and I were once listening to a rock band with her. The next thing I knew she was on the dance floor bouncing to the music with two energetic little girls, who were clearly thrilled to have a grownup not only notice them but also join them in their play.

My friend understands that both animals and children have needs that are not always noticed by grownups, who have what they may consider to be more important business to attend to.

The Samaritan did not, as far as I know, have cat food in his pack.

He did, however, have oil and wine, and he used them to help a hurt man. A man who was not of his kind.

But no matter. Hurt is hurt. Need is need.

And we are called to help. We are called to be ready to help.

Whether we carry food for a hungry animal.

Or medicine to help someone who has been injured.

Or healing words to help patch up a heart that is broken or a soul that is desperate.

May we be ready to help. May we widen the circle to include those whom others neglect.

Questions

1. Have you ever found yourself torn between helping someone and just continuing on your way? Share some examples of those times.

2. Have you ever been in need of help or friendship and felt as if the world was passing you by? Share how that felt to you.

3. What are ways in which we can include more people in our family circle, even people with needs we would rather ignore?

Family Challenge

The next time someone asks you for help of any kind, imagine that person is a member of your family. Then help that person as you would your own brother or sister.

Prayer

O God of mercy and compassion, forgive us when we pass by those in need, whether that need be physical, emotional, or spiritual. Give us the heart of your Son that we might know the true meaning of being a neighbor. Expand our ideas of what *family* is so that we might be a part of your family. In the name of the One who ever expands the family, *our* family, we pray. Amen.

Chapter 7

Jesus

For where two or three are gathered in my name, I am there among them.

— Matthew 18:20

And [Jesus] said to them, "Whoever welcomes this child in my name welcomes me.

— Luke 9:48

I am now rejoicing in my sufferings for your sake, and in my flesh I am completing what is lacking in Christ's afflictions for the sake of his body, that is, the church. I became its servant according to God's commission that was given to me for you, to make the word of God fully known, the mystery that has been hidden throughout the ages and generations but has now been revealed to his saints. To them God chose to make known how great among the Gentiles are the riches of the glory of this mystery, which is Christ in you, the hope of glory.

— Colossians 1:24–27

Jim says . . .

Jesus invited me to her classroom to do a magic show for a group of preschoolers.

I say Jesus, but if pushed I will admit it was Peggy Strunk who gave the invitation.

Miss Peggy, as she is known to children and parents alike, taught three- and four-year-olds for thirty years at Memorial Presbyterian Church in Norman, Oklahoma.

One of my duties as pastor was to show up most years to perform magic for her young students.

Preschoolers are at a great age for a magic show.

The simplest trick by a very amateurish magician elicits a squeal of surprise and, unlike older children, this age group rarely makes any attempt to figure out how the trick is done. For them, the world is still magical and *anything* can happen!

Those children were amazing. Very polite. Very alive. Very interactive. Stars in their eyes and vast dreams in their heads.

Some of them had once been hitters, pinchers, or biters. Some had been withdrawn, ready to cry at the slightest threat. Potential preschool dropouts.

But this Jesus of a woman won their hearts and, with cheerful firmness, opened the window to a more promising future for them.

Never once did my phone ring with a complaining parent on the other end.

If there was ever even one issue, I was not aware of it.

Indeed, I cannot imagine a parent who would object to the Vatican bestowing sainthood on this fine lady.

For she did achieve miracles.

Her constant upbeat way of teaching and leading, her clear alpha voice setting unmistakable boundaries, her passion and love and graciousness—they all played no small part in shaping little people who are now leaders in their communities.

There is a proverb that counsels us to "train up a child" in the way we believe is right (Prov. 22:6, KJV).

Miss Peggy was always training "up" her children, working tirelessly to move them to the next level of development. Although she is no longer teaching, to this day she still has a very up attitude.

For me, she has been a picture of what Christ looks like, only in contemporary garb.

The apostle Paul spoke of the mystery of "Christ in you" (Col. 1:27). No doubt about it. Jesus, the Christ, can be seen in Peggy Strunk.

Jesus was seen and present on those mornings and afternoons when two and more were gathered in Miss Peggy's preschool classroom.

As this teacher opened her arms in welcome to her young charges, she opened that holy space to the presence of Christ.

The result was that every fall a little family came into existence and lived and thrived for nine months. But it did not die, for we all know that we continue to be blessed by those old ties that still bind us one to another.

Thank God for Peggy Strunk.

Thank God for the little missionaries she sent out into the world.

Thank God for the face of Jesus that is seen every day in the human treasures that bless our lives.

Paul says . . .

As a young boy I once asked my dad, "Are you God or Jesus?" He smiled, knowing a great little sermon illustration was unfolding before him.

"Well, in a way I'm both," he told me. "I carry Jesus in my heart, and Jesus carries God. I try to represent Jesus to you. But mainly I'm just your dad."

For better or worse, those of us who profess that we are Christian carry his name. When we love others, Jesus' love is seen and experienced. When we hate others, we do great damage to his reputation.

In *Les Misérables* Victor Hugo wrote, "To love another person is to see the face of God." Jesus is the face of God. As he walked on earth he was the face of God to those he loved.

When a woman caught in the act of adultery was about to be stoned by the men of the village, Jesus intervened. Instead of the judgment she saw in the faces of the other men, in Jesus' face she saw love. She saw compassion, mercy, grace. She saw the face of God.

Show love. Show Jesus. Show God. They are all the same thing.

Questions

1. Who has been Jesus to you? When you were a child? As an adult?

2. What would you say is the key characteristic or trait of Jesus?

3. What is one thing about you that becomes Jesus to others?

Family Challenge

It has been said, "Remember, you are not the Messiah." But it has also been said, "Remember, the Messiah lives among you." Watch for signs of Christ in the people in your life during the coming week. Try to treat others as you believe Christ would treat them.

Prayer

Lord Jesus, you have always welcomed us. You have surrounded us through so many people. In sacrificial ways you have given and given and given your life to each of us. As we reach out to you with a hand, may we be ready to reach out to others with our other hand. Always including, always blessing, always letting the mystery weave its wonders. Amen.

Chapter 8

Chuy

And from there he arose and went away to the region of Tyre and Sidon. And he entered a house and did not want anyone to know, yet he could not be hidden. But immediately a woman whose little daughter had an unclean spirit heard of him and came and fell down at his feet. Now the woman was a Gentile, a Syrophoenician by birth. And she begged him to cast the demon out of her daughter. And he said to her, "Let the children be fed first, for it is not right to take the children's bread and throw it to the dogs." But she answered him, "Yes, Lord; yet even the dogs under the table eat the children's crumbs." And he said to her, "For this statement you may go your way; the demon has left your daughter." And she went home and found the child lying in bed and the demon gone.

— Mark 7:24–30, English Standard Version

Paul says . . .

I did not grow up with dogs. We had cats. Cats are easy. If you leave town for a few days, you just set out extra food and water. If you are gone for a week, then you have your neighbor check in after a few days. Cats come and go as they please. Yes, they can be affectionate, but they do not get carried away with it. Dogs, on the other hand, are aggressively affectionate and require much attention. Frankly, I never thought I would ever have a dog. But I married a dog person who is also allergic to cats.

One day shortly before Christmas, I received a text notification on my phone. It was from my wife, and a photo was attached. I opened it up, and there was my wife holding the sweetest little puppy God has ever made. There was no fighting it. We had a dog.

We named him Chuy, after our favorite Mexican restaurant. Names are important to me. I always like to know what they mean. In the case of the name of our dog, his name had to be about more than Mexican food. As it turns out, *Chuy* is the pet name for "Jesus" in Spanish. I cannot tell you how *Chuy* comes from *Jesus*, but it does, and he does.

Jennifer and I struggled to have children, but to no avail. Chuy filled a place in our hearts that needed filling. He quickly stole our hearts, and he made us a family.

He has also led us into a broader family.

Since we have gotten Chuy, we have been getting to know our neighbors. When you walk a dog, especially one as awesome as ours, neighbors come out of the woodwork. People are just more apt to talk to a person walking a dog than to a person walking alone. People who walk alone are watched cautiously from windows, but walk a dog and somehow you have passed some kind of screening process. I guess people who walk dogs are just more approachable. Easy conversation. Talk about the dog.

One neighbor I have gotten to know is Sam. I had seen Sam working in his yard before and exchanged nods but never introduced myself. One day while walking Chuy, I saw Sam sitting in his garage with the door open. He called me over. Sam is about the easiest person in the world to talk to, and he does not even need a dog to get a conversation going.

We covered all the typical first-time conversational topics: weather, sports, my dog, his kids and grandkids, his retirement, my profession. Telling people I am a minister either kills the conversation or opens it up to very deep levels. Upon hearing what I do, a person's initial response is usually something of a confession, "Well, I haven't been to church in a while." Which was how Sam responded, but he continued, "I am a Christian, though, and I read the Bible regularly. We used to go to church all the time; but then we moved here, and we just haven't found a new one."

We chatted a little more on this subject. He asked about my church and how I had gotten into ministry. I told him about the book I had written that would be out soon, and that got us on the subject of prayer. Just when it looked as if our conversation was coming to a close, he said, "Keep me in your prayers. I'm having knee replacement surgery next Tuesday." I told him about my prayer resolution to never delay when it comes to praying for someone. He smiled and took my hand. He has a strong, athletic hand. I prayed.

Sam ended up delaying his surgery. He just did not feel good about it. We continued to chat whenever I walked by with Chuy. Eventually, he rescheduled his surgery. The week before he was to go in for it, he called me over again. He had a copy of my book and wanted me to sign it. I joked that now it would be worth a penny more.

"No," he said and looked me straight in the eyes. "Now it's priceless."

I said it was sure nice to have such a neighbor.

He corrected me again, "Friend."

Sam's surgery went fine.

One evening, a couple of days after he came home from the hospital, my wife and I were walking with Chuy and, for the first time, our newborn son, Nelson. Sam and his wife, Nancy, came out to greet us on the sidewalk. They were both all smiles. Sam said all the standard yet sincere things you say to new parents. Then he turned to me. "Paul, your book has inspired me. Let me lead us in a prayer." He took my hand, and we all, including Chuy, formed a circle around our beautiful, long-hoped-for child. He prayed. I felt as if we were a family standing around a Thanksgiving Day table, a table prepared by God.

There is always room for more at the table, and no one need eat the crumbs. Chuy will be glad to take care of those.

Jim says . . .

Why was Jesus so unfriendly to the Syrophoenician woman?

> Or was he being a clever rabbi, appearing to be unfriendly until she explained why she, though not a Jew, should be included in what Jesus had to offer?

> Or, as some biblical scholars have suggested, perhaps Jesus was still growing in his understanding of his mission, and this woman actually helped him see that his gifts were not only for the Jews.

Whatever the reason, through the story we come to understand that "dogs" are people, too. Well, to put it a better way, even dogs should be treated with respect.

Our family has always had pets, although our pets have been primarily cats.

After having an overly challenging relationship with a dog earlier in our married life, we never intended to have another. Then one day our youngest son, John, brought home a puppy, a mixture of Labrador Retriever and who knows what else. Her coloring led John to call her Honey.

> John moved out a year or two later. Honey stayed. And, as I write this, she has continued to stay with us for the last fourteen years.

> From Honey we have learned more about ourselves.

>> Perhaps the primary thing I have learned is that there are living beings on our planet who will love us with no strings attached.

>> But not only love us. Honey, even as an old dog, is always excited to see us return home.

>> We may have made only a quick trip to the grocery store. Or we could be returning from a weeklong vacation. It makes no difference how short or long our absence has been.

>>> Honey greets us as if she has not seen us for a million years and is extremely happy we have found our way home to her again. Her tail wags. Her countenance lights up. She is a happy creature.

Does God view us, at least in part, as Honey views my wife and me? Is God always happy to see us?

> What about how we relate to others? Frankly, it is very difficult to consistently welcome people as enthusiastically as Honey consistently welcomes us.

>> Sometimes my welcome is tinged with judgment or indifference. Sometimes I am very picky about whom will receive a warm welcome from me.

Admittedly, dogs can also be picky. But Honey seems to be willing to make friends with everyone who comes around.

Thank God for the blessing of Honey.

Thank God for Jesus, who welcomes us when no one else does.

And thank God for the blessing of that Syrophoenician woman, who welcomed Jesus and, if some biblical scholars are right, may even have helped him understand how far God his Father expected him to open his arms to others.

Questions

1. How have pets played a part in your family life?

2. How have pets connected you to people outside your home?

3. What are ways in which you can be more welcoming to your neighbors? Are you open to doing this?

Family Challenge

Find a way to connect with your neighbors, welcoming them with deep appreciation. If you do not have a dog, consider making cookies. Those are always welcome, too.

Prayer

O Creator of all living creatures, thank you for our pets and all they mean to us. Help us to be open to family in whatever ways you provide it. In Chuy's name we pray. Amen.

Chapter 9

Siri

Don't pick on people, jump on their failures, criticize their faults—unless, of course, you want the same treatment.

— Matthew 7:1–2, *The Message*

And let us consider how to stir up one another to love and good works.

— Hebrews 10:24, English Standard Version

Jim says . . .

In two days I will be heading to Houston, Texas, to see my cousin and his wife. I have never visited them before, but I am confident I will find their home.

> I am confident not because they have given me directions, but because Siri will lead me there.

Siri is the voice I hear from my iPhone when I use my GPS to find a new destination.

> I have learned to trust her.

Sometimes I make a wrong turn. Other times I decide to follow a different path from the one she has prescribed.

> Never once has she said, "Idiot," or, "Trust me, Jim. You don't have to take off on your own."

Always patient. Never chiding. But forever persistent. Determined to get me there even if I choose to go to Alaska before finally aiming for Houston.

One day it struck me. That is how God is. Patient. Persistent. Determined to get me down that Jesus road. Some say God chides. Perhaps that is true. But I have come to realize that chiding does not do much good when I do it. What works for me is to keep nudging and loving and believing that we all get a little closer tomorrow.

> I think I have learned that from watching God. And from paying attention to a handful of people who watch God more closely than I do.

Siri, like God, gives me space to mess up. Siri gives me hope that, in spite of my insistence on getting lost, I will arrive. Perhaps even on time. Or, at least on Siri's time. For Siri keeps recalculating the estimated time of arrival just as some parents recalculate when their children will finally grow up and leave the failure-to-launch stage behind.

There is, however, one way to get lost so that Siri cannot help you.

> It happens when you turn Siri off. She does not turn herself back on.

I think this happens in our life with God as well. When we turn God off, turn away and head out to wherever we insist on going, we will get lost.

> But when we turn back, God is always there. Just as when I turn my iPhone on again and go to my GPS setting, Siri is there, ready to get me going again.

God, unlike Siri, will choose to intervene even when we do not turn back. We may disconnect from God, but God will keep on finding ways to keep connecting with us.

And that is how it is supposed to be with families. We are supposed to keep connecting, keep persisting, keep remembering that "love is patient; love is kind" (1 Cor. 13:4) and showing that patience and kindness to one another.

> Yes, we will slip into judging. Berating. Maybe even shouting and yelling. But it is when we maintain a steady, nonjudgmental face and voice, and keep encouraging those we love to "turn this way, head this way, keep going this way" that the good things happen.

I have read that *Siri* is a Norwegian word that means "beautiful woman who leads you to victory."

> Yes. That is good. That is, in fact, what I have experienced in over forty years of being married to a beautiful, real-life, flesh-and-blood woman who has more than once snatched me from the jaws of defeat.

May we all be a part of beautiful families who are leading one another to victory.

Paul says . . .

I was something of a tender boy and apt to getting picked on from time to time by harsher kids. When this happened, my mother would paraphrase Romans 12:20 to me. "Heap hot coals of kindness on their heads," she would advise. Sometimes she would say, "That boy is probably just really sad."

Both of those statements have made a large impact on how I respond to others and how I view people who act meanly toward me. Bullies turn into people I am to bless and who deep down have been greatly wounded. If we allow other people's actions to determine our own reactions, then we will be led down a dead-end road.

I am grateful God does not act toward me the same way in which I act toward others. Instead, God, knowing my sadness, matches my meanness with kindness.

Questions

1. Who has been a Siri to you?

2. Siri never criticizes. When *is* it appropriate to criticize? What do you do, and what should you do, when someone bullies you?

3. In what ways would the world be different if all of us followed Siri's model?

Family Challenge

Let the coming week be a bite-your-tongue week. Leave criticism behind for those seven days. Be patient, persistent when necessary, and help others reach the destination they have chosen with their life GPS.

Prayer

We thank you, God of grace, for the Siris in our lives. We thank you for those who love us and who resist the need to judge what we do. We thank you that they are there to patiently help us, through what they say and do not say, make the correct turns. May we be Siris to others as we live in the Spirit of Christ. Amen.

Chapter 10

Sunday Dinner

The cup of blessing that we bless, is it not a sharing in the blood of Christ? The bread that we break, is it not a sharing in the body of Christ? Because there is one bread, we who are many are one body, for we all partake of the one bread.

— 1 Corinthians 10:16–17

Paul says . . .

I can still smell the pot roast and baked chicken. One of those two dishes always awaited us when we came home from church. Mom would prepare it before we left and pop it into the oven to cook slowly while we attended Sunday school and the worship service.

Even though it was afternoon when we ate it, we called it Sunday dinner. It would have been too informal to call it lunch. It was more than lunch. It was more like Thanksgiving Dinner. It was the only meal during the week we ate in the formal dining room. The rest of the week we ate at the kitchen table.

This Sunday meal was special. It was the time when we were most a family. The meal was unhurried because the only thing we had to do afterward was have a rest time when we children went to our rooms for an hour or so. My brothers and I never actually slept; we listened to records and played games. In the evening we ate leftovers and watched *The Wonderful World of Disney*.

As my brothers and I grew older, we would invite friends from church to join us. Since we all went to the university in the town we grew up in, we continued to do so into our twenties. We learned from our friends that what our family did was not the norm. We discovered that by being part of our Sunday dinner, our friends felt included in our family. Often they would stay all day because in the evening our church's college group met at our house. We would have a devotional and then transition into watching *Star Trek: The Next Generation*. Lifelong friends developed from this group.

It was always like a party with sometimes as many as a dozen of us crowded around the table. We laughed a lot. In fact, we often sat down at the table in such high spirits we could hardly make it through the blessing without bursting out laughing. We dared not open our eyes because we knew if any of us caught a glance from another, the closing amen had better come quickly.

Church was the same way for me. It was special, like our Sunday family dinner. The sanctuary on Sunday was like our formal dining room. And just as I had to work to stifle my laughter during the blessing of our dinner, so I had to resist the temptation to laugh during the most solemn moments of the worship service.

As an adult, and now the pastor of a church, I realize what an effort my parents put into those Sunday dinners. Such family times did not just happen. It would have been so easy for them to allow the day to be taken over by meetings, work, chores, sports, homework, and separateness. Our Sunday family time required intentionality and preparation.

The better we prepare, the better we enjoy. This means getting work done, doing chores, and paying bills before Sunday. That pot roast does not cook itself! It also means not making other commitments on Sunday. This is becoming harder and harder to do. Many people feel they have no choice but to work on Sunday. They are afraid they will get behind or lose their job. The only business that does not open on Sunday is the liquor store, and it is only a matter of time before it does. Sunday is in danger of becoming just another day, another day in which we are obliged to the world.

What if the day were more like a meal, a special meal? Sunday dinner.

Jim says . . .

Go back with me almost fifty years.

> I was part of a college Christian fellowship that brought in weekly speakers. Our speaker for the week I am remembering here was a pastor from Houston.
>
> I was walking toward the student center when I saw our speaker walking in the same direction. He was about half a block away. I stopped and watched.

He walked along slowly, as if he had no care in the world, as if the only thing on his mind was the time he would spend with us that evening. Unhurried. No hint of distraction. Calm.

The image of that pastor has been a powerful force in my life.

It has helped me strive to live in the present.

One technique I developed as a pastor to help me be in the here and now is called the three-minute focus.

If someone called me as I was getting ready to leave my office for a meeting, I would try to give them my full, unhurried attention for at least three minutes.

Then I would end the conversation and ask that person to please get back with me later if he or she wanted to talk more.

Paul's picture of our Sunday dinner is a metaphor for creating a special time in the present. I have tried to provide the people in my life with ongoing Sunday dinners, even if it is only three unhurried, undistracted, calm minutes on the telephone.

Sunday dinners at our home were part of the way we chose to honor the Sabbath.

They were our way of stopping the rush of life to take time to be with each other.

Time to bless each other with our attention and our good humor while enjoying a delicious meal.

In a world where almost no one creates a full Sabbath day in the traditional sense, it is important to create mini-Sabbaths.

Times during which we slow down or stop, and welcome the present.

It may be a mini-Sabbath you give to yourself. Stopping to read or to nap or to sit quietly in the car for five minutes to munch on the Snickers bar you just bought from the 7-Eleven.

Or it may be the three minutes (or longer) you give to a friend who calls and says, "I know you're probably busy," and you respond, "My only business right now is talking with you."

Questions

1. When was the last day you can remember having zero obligations and doing nothing but enjoying being in the present?

2. Whom did you spend that day with?

3. What would it take for you to make a day like that happen every week?

Family Challenge

Plan a day in the near future that is purely for rest and recreation. Invite others to join you in it. If at all possible, prepare everything in advance. Guard this date carefully on your calendar. Enjoy.

Prayer

O Lord, you are our shepherd. You make us lie down in green pastures, and you lead us beside still waters in order to restore our souls and our relationships. Empower us to embrace the command to take a full day of rest every week, that we might be free from the world and enjoy the good gifts of your creation, which include family. Amen.

Chapter 11

Love

Love is patient; love is kind. . . . It bears all things, believes all things, hopes all things, endures all things.

— 1 Corinthians 13:4, 7

Owe no one anything, except to love one another; for the one who loves another has fulfilled the law.

— Romans 13:8

Jim says . . .

She wandered with purpose through a Borders bookstore. Allison, my granddaughter, was looking for a gift for her mother.

Her mother was in the hospital for the second time in a month, having had a follow-up surgery earlier that day.

Allison, a fifth grader at the time, had eighteen dollars left on a Borders gift card and three dollars in cash.

Her intention was to get something for her mother and something for herself.

She soon found a book, *The Notebook* by Nicholas Sparks. She knew her mother had liked the movie based on the book and thought the book itself would be a good gift.

Allison turned up at the cash register with two items. The book and a package containing three tubes of body lotion, three different scents. Both were gifts for her mom. Nothing for herself. The cashier took her gift card and two of the three dollars Allison had in her hand, returning some coins in change.

As we left the store, the hour now past nine o'clock in the evening, Allison asked if we could stop by the hospital to drop off the gifts for her mother.

One does not simply drop off anything at a hospital. You park your car. You walk to the building. You negotiate the maze that defines every hospital until you finally arrive at the room.

But we went.

Allison's mother was surprised to see us. I myself was surprised to see us there because our original plan had been to head home after our shopping trip and go to the hospital the next morning. But I was aware, from past experience, of the persistence of this young lady.

She already understood the importance of going the extra mile and not waiting until tomorrow to do what will touch another person today.

It was, I suppose, in the grand scheme of things, a small act.

That is, however, what love is: a series of small acts. A word here. A gesture there. An act of kindness that sets one's own desires aside.

And that, I have come to believe, is what it means to live as a Christian.

The love of God finds its way into our heart, and then it goes out from our heart and into the world. Little by little. Day by day. The world is blessed. God's universe is changed.

Paul says . . .

The basic definition of *bless* is to "make holy." It comes from an Old English word meaning to "mark with blood," which pertains to blood sacrifice. The root of the Hebrew word for *blessing* means to "kneel down." It is an act of worship. Today that Hebrew word is most commonly understood as to "make happy."

I must be honest and say that while today's understanding of this word is nice, it is shallow if it is not connected to something like kneeling or sacrifice. A blessing that costs little, blesses little. Perhaps *love* is a better word for "blessing." Love costs. Love kneels. Love sacrifices. It is not enough to say that love makes us happy, but yet, oh, what happiness there is in loving! And oh, what pain there is in loving, as well!

Love gushes forth like blood from a wound. It spills out onto the altar and makes holy all that it marks. It covers over a great many wrongs. It fills a heart and gives life.

Love makes holy. Love blesses. Love makes family.

Questions

1. Who has taught you the most about love? What did that person teach you?

2. How do you see love differently now than when you were a child or a teenager?

3. Why did the apostle Paul say we "owe" love to other people (Rom. 13:8)? Why did he say we owe nothing but love? Does this mean we can forget about our mortgage, our car payment, or our credit card bills?

Family Challenge

Keep a daily record for one week of the kind words and deeds you have said and done for others. Also record the kind words and deeds that have come your way.

Prayer

God of love, Lord of patience, thank you for your daily presence in my life. Help me to keep out of "love debt" by constantly passing on the blessings you have passed to me. May I have eyes tuned to receive the love that comes my way and a heart ready to send words and deeds of love to others. Amen.

Chapter 12

Welcoming

At that time the disciples came to Jesus and asked, "Who is the greatest in the kingdom of heaven?" He called a child, whom he put among them, and said, "Truly I tell you, unless you change and become like children, you will never enter the kingdom of heaven. Whoever becomes humble like this child is the greatest in the kingdom of heaven. Whoever welcomes one such child in my name welcomes me.

— Matthew 18:1–5

Paul says . . .

A few years ago I was taking one of our neighborhood youths to football practice. Wallace is an extremely outgoing young man who has brought more people to our church than just about anyone else. As we got out of the car he said, "Come meet Moses. He lives near the church."

Wallace led me across the field to young Moses, who was a little bigger than the other boys. "This is Pastor Paul," Wallace introduced me. "You should come by the church and play basketball with us."

Moses smiled at me shyly, "Okay."

Moses' family had emigrated from Uganda when he was younger. His accent is still very thick. A lot of the kids mock the way he speaks, but he just smiles as if he enjoys the attention. He has one of the sweetest natures a teenage boy could have. Not only did Moses begin coming to the church to play basketball that summer, but he also became a regular that fall at our youth program.

When the church began holding its confirmation classes the following spring, I approached Moses about it. He told me I would have to speak to his parents. He went on to explain he would need to get his older sister to translate for them because they speak very little English. We agreed upon a time, and I asked Jon, one of the elders of the church, to join me.

Jon and I arrived at Moses' family's house in the late afternoon a few days later. Moses led us into the living room where his sister, mother, and father were sitting. They all rose, and the sister translated their warm greeting and invitation to sit.

Moses' parents were older than I expected. He had been a late-in-life gift to his parents. He has several grown siblings. His parents listened carefully as I explained, through their daughter's translation, the purpose for our visit.

His father responded by telling us Moses had been baptized as a child. He himself was an Anglican minister. He knew about confirmation. He said he would be very glad for Moses to receive instruction and be confirmed in the church.

I told them how impressed we had been with Moses and how much we cared about him.

Then his mother looked at me with a cheerful yet serious expression on her face and said, "In this house, we are his parents. When he is at the church, you are his father. You are our eyes and our ears. Do you understand?"

I was taken aback by the charge but assured her I did understand. Jon nodded his head in agreement.

I asked if I could offer a prayer. Moses' parents said they would be honored if I did. I prayed a prayer of thanks for the incredible goodness they had instilled in their son, and I asked God to continue to bless them as a family. As Jon and I stood up to leave, the mother spoke to her daughter, who then explained her parents would now like to offer a blessing. Of course!

Rising to their feet, they began to clap in rhythm and sing to us with great jubilation. For a moment I felt as if I had been transported to their homeland. I felt thoroughly welcomed. What a gift their blessing was!

It is easy to believe that people have nothing or little to offer. Sometimes those who seem to have the least are really the ones who have the most to give. I do not know who was more blessed, Moses' parents, Jon and I, or Moses; but I do know I was greatly blessed. I have never been given such a beautiful blessing.

Moses continues to be a blessing in my life as I watch him grow into a fine young man. I will always be his church father, the loving eyes and ears of his parents whenever he is in my care.

Christ calls us to welcome each other, and in doing so we will receive great blessing. Imagine a world in which we are always welcome. Imagine how your world would change if you welcomed others into it. In that moment we will be in Christ's homeland.

Jim says . . .

Humility does not come naturally for many of us.

> I certainly was not being humble the day I stood over my son Paul as he sat quietly on a chair in our den.
>
> I was going on and on about some grievance I had with him. As I talked, my sixteen-year-old son, without a word, rose until my gaze was forced to shift upward into the face of someone who was already a couple of inches taller than I.
>
> There was no expression of hostility or aggression on his face. He said not a word. He did not have to.
>
> The message was clear. He was no longer a little boy. I instantly realized I was talking to a young man.

When one's son moves from boyhood to manhood there is an important decision to be made.

Will I welcome him into my life in a different way?

> Will I do what I need to do to move from being a father to a little kid to being a father to an adult child?

One of the great joys of my life is the way Paul has welcomed me into his adult life.

In his work as a Presbyterian pastor, he has welcomed my cheerleading (one of a parent's number one responsibilities), and he has taken the initiative in asking for and welcoming words of advice from me about his ministry.

As he has entrusted himself to me, I have been aware of how careful I must be not to betray that trust.

I am not there to criticize. But when invited, I can offer observations that might be helpful.

The fun thing about it all is that we talk, sometimes endlessly, about ministry in a way that allows us both to learn from each other.

"Oh, Lord, it's hard to be humble," as the country singer-songwriter Mac Davis has cried.

It is hard. But it is much more rewarding than being domineering and arrogant.

And being humble leads to blessings I would never have anticipated receiving.

Questions

1. In what ways have you been welcomed?
2. How have you welcomed others?
3. In what ways could you be more welcoming?

Family Challenge

Welcome new people into your life and receive whatever blessing they wish to give to you. Make them part of your family and become part of theirs.

Prayer

O God of welcome, you always receive us with open arms. You are the great host! Help us to welcome others and to be your eyes and ears for those you have entrusted to us. Amen.

Chapter 13

Church

But you are a chosen people, a royal priesthood, a holy nation, God's possession, that you may declare the praises of him who called you out of darkness into his wonderful light.

— 1 Peter 2:9, New International Version

Let the message of Christ dwell among you richly as you teach and admonish one another with all wisdom through psalms, hymns, and songs from the Spirit, singing to God with gratitude in your hearts.

— Colossians 3:16, New International Version

He said to them, "Therefore every teacher of the law who has become a disciple in the kingdom of heaven is like the owner of a house who brings out of his storeroom new treasures as well as old."

— Matthew 13:52, New International Version

Jim says . . .

A Sunday school teacher once told me she asked a group of children, "What do you think of when you hear the word *church*?"

One girl, age ten or thereabouts, replied, "A place to learn new things."

How much I have learned from children over the years!

They see things through eyes fresher than mine.

Their words may be words I have heard before, but often they are ones I have forgotten or set aside or left behind.

I remember one day when our son David, who was maybe six at the time, announced to us at the dinner table that he knew God's color.

"What color is God?" we asked.

"Gray," David answered, in complete seriousness.

"Gray?" we echoed. "Where did you hear that?"

And David told us, "God is gray, God is good. Let us thank him for our food."

Ever since then David's words have been a reminder to me that God is indeed more gray than black and white. There is always a certain ambiguity in this God, who can never be pinned down by us.

I have learned much about God from many people and in many places. But I come back to what the little girl said: church is "a place to learn new things."

So many things I have learned in the church.

> The church has taught me compassion and commitment. It has taught me how to let go of stuff that does me no good to hold on to. It has been a laboratory where I sometimes fail and sometimes succeed but where I am always learning.

There are other places in which a person can learn new things, but it is the church that gives me so much of what I need to fill the storerooms of my life.

> The church gives me songs to sing, prayers to pray, and words to shape my life.

> The church gives me people, all kinds of people. People to love. People with whom I sometimes struggle. People who teach me so much. Who bring out "new treasures as well as old" that feed my spirit (Matt. 13:52, NIV).

To learn is to become educated. The word *educate* comes from the Latin *educere*, which means "to draw out."

> That is what the church has done for me. It has drawn me out. It has pulled me out of myself. It has pulled out the good in me. It has shown me the heart of God and is pulling me into that great and good heart.

I thank this young disciple for teaching me through her take on the church. I thank David for teaching me through his take on the color of God.

> Their words have drawn me out a little further as I walk with this "royal priesthood," this "holy nation," this "people belonging to God" (1 Pet. 2:9).

> Together we bless one another as we strive to "teach and admonish one another with all wisdom" (Col. 3:16, NIV).

> Young and old, we draw out the best God has embedded within us.

Paul says . . .

I first saw the man in faded blue scrubs chatting away at the nurse's station as I walked through the secure double doors on my way to pray with Jo, the parishioner I introduced in chapter 2, who was now awaiting another surgery. Whatever he was saying was making the nurse chuckle. He walked on down the hallway, talking amiably to people as he went.

I found my parishioner's room and entered, still amused by the man who was leaving happy people in his wake. While I was visiting with Jo, he came in to prepare her to be rolled into surgery. Jo is a chatter as well and has never known a stranger in her life. She introduced herself and then pointed at me, "This is my pastor."

His eyes lit up. "I'm Willie, Pastor. It does my heart good to know there's a pastor here today. Sure does. Lemme shake your hand." We shook. "Yes, sir. It is *good* to have a pastor here today. Remember Willie when you pray, because I sure do need it." I promised I would not forget.

"Would you also remember my daughter?" he added. "They got her here today, too." His perpetual smile suddenly wavered. "Pastor, they think she tried to take her own life, but I don't believe it. Remember her when you pray, too."

I took Jo's hand and prayed for her surgery. We then prayed for Willie and his daughter.

Later in the recovery room, as Jo was coming to, Willie came in, chatting away with the other hospital employees. I could tell they liked him. He left smiles everywhere he went. When he saw me, he came right over. "Pastor, I know you prayed for me and my daughter. I *felt* it. I thank you kindly, Pastor. Yes, my daughter's doing just fine. I think she's going to be just fine. Good to have a pastor here today. God is good."

"All the time," I responded.

A nurse overheard us and said, "I know you're talking about my Father."

Willie corrected her. "No. He's talking about *our* Father."

Church is wherever and whenever we recognize this is true.

Questions

1. What are one or two of the most important things you have learned from being part of a church?

2. How are you different today than you were as a young adult or as a child? What part has the church played in that difference?

3. Churches are not blessings to everyone. Sometimes they are bad news. What is one thing every church should strive to do that would make churches more of a blessing to the world?

Family Challenge

During the next four Sundays that you attend church, write down one thing you have learned or relearned as a consequence of being at church that day.

Prayer

God of a gathered people, we thank you that we are not alone on this planet. We thank you for others who share the faith, hope, and love you give so abundantly to us. May we bless others by drawing out what is good and excellent and beautiful in them. And may we be constantly drawn into that great fellowship you have promised will one day have no bounds. Amen.

Chapter 14

Budapest

So he came and proclaimed peace to you who were far off and peace to those who were near; for through him both of us have access in one Spirit to the Father. So then you are no longer strangers and aliens, but you are citizens with the saints and also members of the household of God, built upon the foundation of the apostles and prophets, with Christ Jesus himself as the cornerstone. In him the whole structure is joined together and grows into a holy temple in the Lord; in whom you also are built together spiritually into a dwelling place for God.

— Ephesians 2:17–22

Paul says . . .

Every Thursday I pray with a group of pastors and missionaries from a variety of denominational backgrounds. One of the closest friends I have made in this group is a retired Southern Baptist minister named Sim. At a recent gathering Sim shared the following story, and I asked if he might write it up that I could share it with others.

You never know who may be sitting next to you at church or in some other public place. One morning my wife, Betty, and I noticed a young man sitting by himself in our church sanctuary during a morning worship service.

We went over to meet him after the service. He was Tamas, a Vanderbilt University computer science graduate student from Hungary. We took him out to lunch for his first taste of Southern barbecue, and a new friendship was launched.

A lifelong member of the Reformed Church of Hungary back in Budapest, he had visited our downtown Nashville Baptist church to learn more about the Baptist faith. He was in love with Reka, a Baptist girl back home.

Tamas attended our church almost every Sunday. We always greeted him and several times invited him to our house for a home-cooked American meal. He loved it and liked being with us. He and I were also able to go to a Mexican restaurant near campus a few times during the year. He would talk about Reka, his studies, and his life in general.

I had started an international stamp collection ministry through the church as a way to connect with people from other countries who are living in our city. I asked Tamas if he could get me some stamps from Hungary. "I think so," he said. "My mother collects them." Over the year, he gave me several hundred Hungarian stamps, many of which were professionally mounted.

Toward the end of the year, Tamas started urging us to come see Budapest. He even gave us a book of the sights to see in his city. My wife and I had been to England, France, and Germany but never to Eastern Europe.

For a large part of my life Eastern Europe meant communism. The Iron Curtain separated our worlds. We were the good guys, and they were the bad guys. Would I now be traveling to such a place as a guest? The idea grew on us, and we began to make plans to go there.

First we went sightseeing in Prague and Vienna, and then we took the train to Budapest. Tamas and Reka met us at the train station, took us to our hotel, and then began showing us their hometown. We arrived as strangers in a strange land, and they served as our guides, giving up four days of their life to show us around.

After the Sunday morning worship service at their church, they took us to Tamas's boyhood home for a home-cooked Hungarian meal with his parents and brother. We had a great meal and a great time. His mother gave us gifts of embroidery for Betty and Hungarian stamps for me. Later the next day Tamas asked us if his parents could take us to a favorite restaurant in Budapest. It was an offer we were glad to accept.

During the meal, Tamas and the women were able to talk with each other fairly easily. At my end of the table, I could converse with his brother, who spoke English quite well. But I could only nod and gesture to his dad, with very limited conversation occurring between us.

At the end of the meal, as we walked back to where the cars were parked, his dad stopped me and looked at me, face-to-face and man-to-man. He then said in perfect English and with genuine feeling, "I want to thank you and your wife for the spiritual blessing you were to my son at an important time in his life."

That is the only English Tamas's dad was ever able to say to me, and it was clear he had carefully learned and practiced this short speech for my sake. What a blessing it has been to my life!

It sure is great to know we have family in Budapest.

Not only would it never have occurred to Sim to go to Budapest, but it was beyond his imagination that he and his wife would form such a deep relationship with a family there. The time invested in welcoming a young stranger to the United States led to incredible blessing for two families, now one family. All because of a shared faith, stamp collecting, and blessing.

ఆ ళ

We live in remarkable times. At any given moment we might meet a person from the other side of the world. If we choose to initiate a relationship, a faraway place is brought near to us in that person. The world is being connected through such relationships. A worldwide family is being created by the universal Spirit of humanity's Father, God.

In the Temple of Jerusalem, which was destroyed in the first century, a giant curtain partitioned off the place called the Holy of Holies. It was recognized that the presence of God was so palpable in that space that it was too dangerous for anyone to go into it. Only the high priest entered and only once a year. The other priests tied a rope to his ankle so they could pull him out if the Lord struck him down. It was reported that at the moment Jesus died on the cross, the curtain was mysteriously torn from top to bottom (Matt. 27:50–51; Mark 15:37–38). Christ's death opened the way to God.

There will be a day when all the curtains that divide us will be torn down and the way will be opened for all humanity to dwell together as one family. In fact, the way has already been made. Christ has shown it to us: "love one another" (John 13:34, 15:12).

Have you ever considered you might also have family in Budapest?

Jim says . . .

When I came to Norman, Oklahoma, in 1984 to be the pastor of Memorial Presbyterian Church, I soon met Martin and Sarah.

Martin was from Cameroon, and Sarah was from the United States.

This biracial couple, who had grown up in different countries, as well as their three sons, were an integral part of our church.

Sarah became famous for ending our church's participation in a softball league when a ball hit her on the nose one day and blood gushed forth.

For several members of what was becoming an aging team, that was enough.

A couple of years later Clarisse showed up. Clarisse, we learned, was Martin's daughter from a previous wife.

She instantly became a part of the church's youth group, and her lively, outgoing nature won the hearts of her new friends.

As the years passed, other African families became a part of the church.

A student from Nigeria joined us and shared his beautiful voice with the choir for the time it took him to complete his doctoral project and move on.

A young man from Uganda arrived and was plucked from the hands of the police as they prepared to arrest him because he was unable to pay his hotel bill (the church paid it). The church helped him earn his degree from the University of Oklahoma.

> He returned to his country and used his education to offer needed leadership to his people.

Claude from the Democratic Republic of the Congo arrived. A member of his country's United Nations team, he had been a mover and a shaker in his homeland.

> A couple of years later, Claude's wife, Marianne, and their six children got off an airplane and were met in a joyous reception by church members.

It may not know about Budapest, but Memorial Presbyterian Church has become a home for many who have come from a variety of African nations.

> The church has helped these people when called upon, and the church has been blessed by the constant reminder that we live in a much bigger world than Oklahoma or even the United States of America.

None of us will forget the chilling day when ten-year-old William, who had been born in Cameroon, was hit by a car as he was crossing the street after a visit to a 7-Eleven.

> For days he was in critical condition. For weeks his progress toward recovery was steady but very slow.

>> For years he continued to have a number of problems arising from the injury.

> The church, led by many people in many ways, rallied behind

William and his family.

> William became a living testimony to the ties that bind us one to another. He is doing fine now. He has graduated from high school and gone on to attend college in Texas.

We may not have to go looking for Budapest. But we do need to be ready to welcome Budapest, with open hearts and hands, when it drops into our laps.

Questions

1. What connections do you have to other parts of the world?
2. How might you take those relationships to a deeper level?
3. What blessing do you have to offer to those who are strangers in this land?

Family Challenge

Consider showing a foreigner your hometown. Be sure to share a meal together. Families are often created around dinner tables.

Prayer

O Creator of all, though the world seems far off to us, you are near to it all. Draw us all closer together through our relationships, so that the world may one day be a family with you as its Father. In Christ, the Great Connector, we pray. Amen.

Chapter 15

Salvation

The wolf shall live with the lamb,
> the leopard shall lie down with the kid,

the calf and the lion and the fatling together,
> and a little child shall lead them.

> — Isaiah 11:6

And if anyone forces you to go one mile, go also the second mile.

> — Matthew 5:41

Give, and it will be given to you.

> — Luke 6:38

Jim says . . .

Our grandson Kieran loves his Grannie, my wife, Judy.

One day when Kieran was two years old, his Grannie fell. She did not hurt herself, but Kieran did not know that.

> When he realized she had fallen, he hurried over to her. Looked at her closely, and peered into her face.
>
> "Are you hurt, Grannie?" he asked, with intense concern.

Salvation is about caring. Salvation is about giving of yourself so that others may have life.

> Of course, one may wonder how truly caring and giving a two-year-old child is able to be, but it is how Kieran seems to be wired. As he grows, he continues to surprise me.
>
> > Now and then he turns to me and says, "I love you, Papa." Whether he knows what he is really doing or not, I feel the words of God coming through him with a degree of authenticity that keeps me alive.

ಲ ಅ

Earl Hutchison was eighty-three years old when he died. He was a good friend to our son Paul and a member of Priest Lake Presbyterian Church where Paul is the pastor.

When Paul arrived in Nashville, Earl took him under his wing.

> He was a man full of life and good will, both of which he gave generously to Paul.

Earl was a golfer, and he and Paul golfed regularly. Their last round was played one week before he died.

> Whenever they golfed, Earl would listen and offer the wisdom he had acquired from his life experiences. Perhaps there was "Bible" talk. There was always "life" talk.
>
>> Through Earl's gift of himself to Paul, he was, I believe, offering Paul the cup of salvation. He was offering my son the model of a life that helps lead a person to salvation.
>
> Earl did not hit the ball very far. But he was consistent. Always moving toward the green.

He was always moving toward people as well. And he was consistent in moving toward God.

> Paul said that Earl was "ready to live, ready to die, and ready for God."

Earl was a man who showed up.

> He had three children, ten grandchildren, and thirteen great-grandchildren. All of them live in the area, and Earl had the habit of visiting each of them on their birthday.
>
> He also showed up at his church and outside of the church, making it his mission to be present in the world beyond his immediate family. To give of his time, energy, attention—his life—so that others, even strangers, could also have life.

Earl was not a man to let you out of his sights.

> If you were in his circle, which was a pretty big one, you stayed in his thoughts, in his prayers, and in the warmth of his heart.

Earl showed up in my life, and I miss him. His spirit touched my spirit.

What was it about him that captured me? Was it any one thing he said? Was it his infectious laugh? Was it his aura of peacefulness, his listening ear?

> Upon reflection, it was the feeling of being in the presence of someone who cared about me, who was interested in what I was doing, who had the gift of knowing when to speak and when not to speak.

> It was the feeling of being in the presence of Christ.

When I was with Earl, I believed I was with someone who was giving me life.

> That is how it is when you connect, however briefly, with a person in whom Christ richly dwells.

> That is also how it is when you are in touch with the salvation of God. Which comes, often as not, through people who give of themselves so that others may have life.

※ ※

We say that Jesus died on the cross to save us. That is true.

> But Jesus was also saving us in the days and years leading up to the cross, as he gave of himself so that others could have life.

> So that others could become whole.

> So that others could live in this world in a measure of peace, *shalom*.

> So that others could be prepared to live as life-giving neighbors with God and others throughout eternity.

Whether seen through the caring acts of a two-year-old child or an eighty-three-year-old man, God's salvation is always nearby. Through the people around us—through their listening ears, careful words, and sacrificial acts—God leads us out of our darkest days and our darkest deeds into the light and life of the Way of Jesus.

We are called to receive. We are called to give.

> We are called to choose life and not death, blessings and not curses.
>
>> We are called to be changed. And together, we are called to change the world through the blessings we offer.

Paul says . . .

I once spoke at a workshop held in a small church in a neighborhood that most of its city has abandoned. Paradoxically, you can see the state capitol building from the parking lot of the church building. I doubt, though, the folks at the capitol can see that church.

Most of the members no longer live in the neighborhood, but they feel called to serve and worship there. They look out as best they can for the children and families who live in the neighborhood. That building and its congregation stand as a visible reminder that God has not abandoned the neighborhood.

Throughout the workshop the members of the congregation shared their own stories. One woman told me of an elderly woman in the neighborhood who, for the last forty years or so, has regularly stood out on the street corner to pray for people. As children walk by she calls out, "Come over here, child! You need some prayer." She then lifts up prayers for them and their families. Even adults walking by receive her attention. "I know you need some prayer for something! Come on over here!"

Over time the neighborhood has become accustomed to coming to her for prayer. She is like the local priest right there on the corner.

Grown men come by and tell her how they remember her praying for them as boys and what it meant to them.

Through the years she has probably prayed for thousands of people. Imagine what she means to her neighborhood. Like the church, she stands as a visible sign that God has not forsaken her neighborhood. How different she is from the street corner preachers I have run across over the years who randomly fire out all the ways a person may be going to hell.

This woman is a street corner pray-er, lifting her people up to God with tears and smiles. Although I will probably never meet her, I can imagine her. Her face is worn with care. Her back is stooped, and her knees are knobby and rough. Her hands are leathery and warm from the sun. Her eyes are like small pools of tears, though there is a light that shines through them with hope. She always sees you before you see her. And she is waiting, always waiting for you to turn the corner.

She reminds me of salvation.

Questions

1. How have you been given life by a child? By an elderly woman or an elderly man?

2. In what ways have you walked the second mile for someone else? How has God walked the second, third, fourth, millionth mile for you?

3. How can you bless and give life to someone in this coming week?

Family Challenge

Think of a person who is in trouble, who is lost in some way. Make it your mission to find ways to specifically bless and give life to this person.

Prayer

Lord Jesus Christ, with every breath you gave life to others. You met broken people and put them back together. You have reached out to us with your saving love. Lead us into ways of giving life to others, no matter how many miles we have to travel. In the power of the Spirit of God we pray. Amen.

Chapter 16

Adoption

But when the fullness of time had come, God sent his Son, born of a woman, born under the law, in order to redeem those who were under the law, so that we might receive adoption as children. And because you are children, God has sent the Spirit of his Son into our hearts, crying, "Abba! Father!" So you are no longer a slave but a child, and if a child then also an heir, through God.

— Galatians 4:4–7

Paul says . . .

Our quest for a child has probably taught my wife and me more about prayer than any other thing we have experienced. We, along with many other people who struggle to have children, prayed for years for a child and were tested in so many ways. We had to learn to trust—really trust—that God is good and loves us. There were some days when this was really hard to believe.

We decided to pursue adoption.

After going through all the necessary steps in the process, we were approved to be on the list of waiting families. We were prepared for another long wait. No problem. What's another year, or three?

The very day we were approved we were told of a couple who had decided upon adoption for their child. The child's delivery was scheduled for the last Tuesday of the month. We were cautiously optimistic. The couple would be shown five profiles, including ours. Not bad odds, if you ask me. It was all in God's hands anyway. We had long ago accepted that.

The due date came and went. We did not hear anything. We prayed for the parents and the child and hoped for a safe delivery. Wednesday, no call. Thursday, no call.

Then Friday came. The phone rang and the caller ID told me it was the agency. My heart began to race. The agency counselor's voice sounded hopeful. The couple wanted to meet with us the next Wednesday.

The delivery had gone fine and as scheduled. A baby boy had been born. Could he be ours, I wondered?

The kind of adoption we had signed up for is called an open adoption, which essentially means the birth parent(s) desires to maintain some level of relationship with the child and the adoptive parents. Most of the time this means the birth mother. The biological father is usually not in the picture. So I was not expecting to be meeting with a couple, especially a married couple not that much younger than us.

The new father greeted us warmly. He knew our profile and history inside and out. In contrast, the mother was very quiet and reserved. At one point he said to her, "Honey, I feel like I'm doing all the talking."

She responded with a shy duck of her head, "That's what I married you for."

We all hit it off. We talked for over three hours with barely a pause. It was odd to think that this couple, not just their child, could be a part of our life from here on out. We liked them from the beginning.

They were going to meet with another couple as well, so they could not make a decision yet. As we were beginning to leave, I offered to pray. The father's face lit up. "Absolutely! That's exactly what we should do."

In the room with us were two agency counselors. As I reached out to take one of the counselor's hands, she hesitated. "Is it okay to include a Jew in the prayer?" Of course!

I prayed for the child and the couple and for wisdom for the difficult decision before them. I prayed for the counselors and for Jennifer and me as well. When we said "Amen," we were all reaching for tissues, including our new Jewish friend.

There was a feeling that God was in charge of this. Whatever happened would be right.

A few days later Jennifer got a call from the agency. The couple wanted to meet with us again.

After we arrived, we all chatted some more as before, but then the father grew serious. He took his wife out of the room with him. In a few minutes they returned. He pulled a laptop out of his bag, opened it, and put it on my lap. On the screen was a letter. He instructed me to read it. It began, "Congratulations, Paul and Jennifer! We have chosen you to be the proud parents of our son." Wow!

After reading this amazing news, I had no words. My wife was holding my hand very tightly. The father stood up and said, "It's my turn to pray." And what a prayer it was! What a man of faith he is. In the prayer he spoke of *our* new family. Four parents, one son, and a whole lot of love.

Two hours later we took our son, Nelson, home.

ೞ ೫

We send news and photos regularly to our fellow parents. Our new family is doing great. Every time I look at Nelson I see not only his birth parents' faces and our own faces in his expressions, I see the loving face of *our* Father smiling back at us.

Adoption has taught me a lot about God's love for me and for others. Adoption is a choice. God has only one begotten son, Jesus Christ. The rest of us are adopted, not because we chose to be adopted but because God chose to adopt us. God saw each one of us and said, "I want you as my own." God chose us and did not leave us orphaned.

Another thing I have learned through adoption about God's love is that, although adoption is the process by which we become God's children, we are not God's *adopted* children. We are God's *children*. The covenant has been eternally established. There is no such thing as unadoption.

It is hard to explain, but when I look at my son, I see just my son. I do not see my adopted son. He is my son as truly as if he had come from my wife and me biologically. He has my heart, and I love him so much it hurts.

Then I think of God my Father and know how he feels about me. It overwhelms me.

Then I look at a stranger on the street and know how God feels about that person as well.

Now, I have a choice to make. Do I choose to recognize that stranger on the street as a member of the same family I was adopted into? Do I choose to bless others by loving them?

God has a family plan. God's family is being created blessing by blessing as we choose to be in relationship with all those whom he has chosen to be part of his family. He will leave no one orphaned. And when the fullness of time comes, God will once again send his Son, our brother, to lead God's family home.

Jim says . . .

Ronnie is my adopted brother.

Now let me explain. My parents did not adopt Ronnie. I did.

One definition of *adopt* is "to take as one's own." That is what I am talking about here. I have a lovely sister, and we are very good friends. But I have no brother. So years ago I chose to adopt Ronnie as my brother.

I say *chose*, but actually our relationship began in a happening sort of way. I was a graduate student, substitute teaching for one of my research adviser's classes. Ronnie was in that class and came up afterward to talk about something I had said.

Exactly what happened next I do not know. What I do know is that we began spending time together, and we have never stopped.

We can be hard on each other's health because when we get together we cannot seem to quit talking until the very wee hours of the morning. Back in our graduate school days that was okay. But at age seventy . . .

We talk about everything—science, politics, Texas, and Oklahoma (Ronnie is Texan up and down and through and through). We talk about God.

> We agree. We disagree. We challenge each other. We learn from each other. Not always bound by what we think and believe, we are always bound by our brotherhood and friendship.

Adopting Ronnie has been easy. He has always treated me with goodness and respect.

> It is not always like that when you adopt a child. When Paul and Jennifer adopted Nelson, they did not know what the future would bring.

>> But they knew they would give themselves to Nelson and help him grow into a mature human being, no matter what challenges and obstacles would come their way.

When God chooses to adopt us into God's kingdom, God does so knowing that things will get pretty rough with some of us.

> God knows that some of us will be very hard to handle and may never show God the appreciation that is due.

How blessed I am to have Ronnie in my life who brings me consistent joy and happiness.

> But how more greatly blessed I am that God, knowing how rebellious I can be, has never chosen to revoke my adoption

papers and say, "Please, take him back. He's too much for me to manage."

Questions

1. How have you been adopted in your life?

2. Whom have you adopted to be a part of your family?

3. What role can you play in creating God's family?

Family Challenge

Live as if every person you encounter is your brother and sister.

Prayer

"Our Father which art in Heaven, Hallowed be thy name. Thy kingdom come. Thy will be done in earth, as it is in heaven. Give us this day our daily bread. And forgive us our debts, as we forgive our debtors. And lead us not into temptation, but deliver us from evil: For thine is the kingdom, and the power, and the glory, forever." Amen (Matt. 6:9–13, KJV).

Chapter 17

Death

O death, where is thy sting?

— 1 Corinthians 15:55, King James Version

Jim says . . .

The phone call came at eight o'clock on a Thursday morning. Mitchell, my sister's son, had been hit by a car. It was serious. His parents had rushed to the hospital.

I immediately got up from my desk at the church and went into the sanctuary. Sat down. Prayed. "God, please help Mitchell be okay."

A voice, clear as a bell, entered my head. "I can't."

Was this the voice of God? Is there anything God cannot do? To this day, I cannot be certain where the voice came from. From God, or from my own self?

Later that morning another call came. Mitchell, age twelve, had died in the hospital.

The apostle Paul wrote, "O death, where is thy sting?" (1 Cor. 15:55, KJV) The implication is that, in Christ, the sting of death is overcome.

But on that day, and for many days afterward, the sting was overwhelming. It was more than a sting. It was a crushing, devastating blow. It was a flood that would not cease.

My wife and I went to the middle school our twin sons, Paul and David, attended, and picked them up. Then we picked up our first-grade son, John, at his school. We took them home. Sat down in the living room with them.

And told them their cousin had been killed.

Paul and David were in the same grade as Mitchell. Mitchell had been born almost seven months after them.

Although we were always separated by many miles, every time our families got together it was like an instant reunion between those three boys. They laughed, they giggled, they were like three brothers together.

Death stings. Death hurts. Death sometimes shuts people still living off from each other. How can a husband and wife address the death of a twelve-year-old? How can they go on? Some do. Some do not.

☙ ❧

Years later my wife and I, along with her sister and our son David, gathered around the bed of Ben Clements, my wife's father. Ben, a World War II Air Force pilot, was almost eighty-six years old. He had recently been diagnosed with cancer. It had spread quickly.

> David drew close to his grandfather. Spoke gently to him, though there was no sign he was heard. As we watched, our son walked with Ben to the door we call death and saw him through it.
>
> Calm. Peaceful. A quiet ending.

Some deaths sting . . . and worse. Other deaths, however, call on us to say, "It was time."

> We go forth thanking God for a person who grew up and did those things we hope to do and expect life to offer us.

Those who gathered around my father-in-law's bed experienced a blessing encounter.

> We left the assisted living facility in the middle of the night knowing we had experienced something special. We now had the memory of having said good-bye at the very moment someone dear to us left this earth.

There were blessings also in the days following Mitchell's death.

We were blessed by the astounding outpouring of love and compassion from family and friends.

We were blessed as we gathered at St. George Episcopal Church and thought about what this young man had given to so many during his brief time with us.

❦ ❧

I have been blessed when I am reminded to try to see each day as *The* day the Lord is giving me and to see each person I encounter as *The* person I am called to be within the moment.

Life ends. Whether twelve years old or eighty-six years old, life ends.

Short or long, the question to me is: What will I do with the time I have? Just as every book ends with a period, so will my life.

For me, at the age of seventy as I write this, I feel the period drawing closer. Each day is precious. How will I use this day and whatever future days I might have?

Knowing death is coming helps me answer this question, adds gravity to my answer.

For me, the sting of death has not yet been vanquished. Knowing, however, how hurtful death can be is teaching me not to sting others with death deeds and death words, those actions and speech that pull people away from life.

Learning from death is, perhaps, a matter of life and death.

Paul says . . .

Jennifer, Nelson, and I recently took a road trip to visit friends and family in the Texas Hill Country. One of our stops along the way was our former home of Austin, primarily to visit a retired pastor and his wife.

We had met John and Theresa through the church we attended while I was in seminary. They are truly two of the most welcoming people I have ever met. No one in need of a greeting ever escaped John's eye, and he had a way of making people feel as if they belonged and mattered. Theresa may just be the greatest hugger of all time. She hugs with the love of Christ, and I feel it every time.

When I learned John had been diagnosed with cancer, I followed his progress through Facebook. It seemed as if treatments were going well, and he and Theresa were hopeful. While I was in Austin for a lecture series some time after his diagnosis, I spotted John and Theresa in the chapel amid the crowd. Although they greeted me as warmly as ever, their faces revealed all was not well. They had just learned John's treatments had been ineffective. There was nothing else that could be done.

The three of us embraced, and we shared a brief prayer.

So here we were, several months later, making our way from Houston to Austin, Nelson sleeping soundly in his car seat. I asked Jennifer to call ahead to let John and Theresa know what time we would arrive, but their grown daughter, Rachel, answered instead. Jennifer listened quietly and then said, "I'm pretty sure Paul is going to want to come anyway."

John had taken a turn for the worse that morning. He had been unresponsive all day, and it would not be long. Jennifer and I wondered if it might be better not to intrude on the family. But as we drove, I began to sense God had a purpose for us being there.

☯ ☪

A support system of close friends and family were chatting in subdued voices when we entered. Rachel greeted me with an anxious hug and led me to her parents' bedroom. "I'm glad you're here, and I know Mom will be, too."

Theresa lay next to her husband, whose breathing was greatly labored. Her face was raw with emotion, and I saw fear in her eyes. She looked weak. She called me to her side, and we hugged. I was welcomed. She wept.

"Paul," she said, "Please talk with him. They told me he can still hear." I went to John's side and told him I had made it, and Jennifer and Nelson were here as well. No response. Theresa said, "Please pray with us."

She placed her hand on John's, and I placed my hand on theirs. I prayed for a peaceful and painless passing through the waters. As I said amen, Rachel led Jennifer, holding Nelson, into the room. Theresa's face lit up, and she rose and greeted Jennifer, her eyes feasting on Nelson. "Oh, my! He's darling," she exclaimed, her face lighting up as Nelson reached for her over Jennifer's arms. "I want to hold him. Let's go into the other room so I can sit down with him."

She sat on the sofa, and Jennifer placed Nelson on her lap. The color seemed to return to Theresa's face and joy to her eyes. She bounced Nelson on her knees and talked to him. He charmed her with happy little coos and giggles.

About twenty minutes later, Rachel went in to check on her father. She reappeared in a moment, crying out, "It's happened! He's gone!" Her legs buckled, and she sat down abruptly and began to sob. Theresa quickly handed Nelson to me and rushed to their bedroom. But John was gone.

Theresa had been so diligent about being by John's side so that she would be present when he passed, but in the end, she had not been present. In a moment he had slipped away.

Her support system of family and friends sprang into action. One called the hospice. Two stayed close to Theresa and Rachel to give total support. Another called the pastor. They all knew their roles. My role, though, was done. I had provided John with a final blessing of presence, allowing him the assurance of knowing his family was not alone in the moment of his passing through to life eternal. That is what we are all doing: just passing through. But the stops we make along the way matter.

Questions

1. What death has stung you the most?

2. What can you learn from knowing that you will die?

3. What have you done recently to bring life to people who are living in a world filled with death deeds and death words?

Family Challenge

Go to a print or online newspaper and read several obituaries. Even if you do not know the person who has died, spend time with the obituary, giving thanks for the person whose life has ended and praying for that person's family.

Prayer

God of life, who has created a world that allows death to flourish, we ask that you teach us and lead us to fill the world around us with life words and life deeds. We pray that the sting of death will remind us to number our own days and live them one by one with purpose and grace and joy. In the Spirit of Christ we pray. Amen.

Chapter 18

Resurrection

When it was evening on that day, the first day of the week, and the doors of the house where the disciples had met were locked for fear of the Jews, Jesus came and stood among them and said, "Peace be with you." After he said this, he showed them his hands and his side. Then the disciples rejoiced when they saw the Lord. Jesus said to them again, "Peace be with you. As the Father has sent me, so I send you." When he had said this, he breathed on them and said to them, "Receive the Holy Spirit. If you forgive the sins of any, they are forgiven them; if you retain the sins of any, they are retained."

But Thomas (who was called the Twin), one of the twelve, was not with them when Jesus came. So the other disciples told him, "We have seen the Lord." But he said to them, "Unless I see the mark of the nails in his hands, and put my finger in the mark of the nails and my hand in his side, I will not believe."

A week later his disciples were again in the house, and Thomas was with them. Although the doors were shut, Jesus came and stood among them and said, "Peace be with you." Then he said to Thomas, "Put your finger here and see my hands. Reach out your hand and put it in my side. Do not doubt but believe." Thomas answered him, "My Lord and my God!" Jesus said to him, "Have you believed because you have seen me? Blessed are those who have not seen and yet have come to believe."

— John 20:19–29

Paul says . . .

Sometimes something happens that is so incredible I find it hard to write about it. I still sit here amazed by the miracle I witnessed. I will do my best to tell you this story truthfully and faithfully. This is how it happened.

A few years ago Mike went to the hospital with a minor infection. When I arrived to pray with him and his wife, Jo, it was clear Mike's mind was not right. Yes, he was already suffering from a variety of mental and emotional challenges, but this was different. This was dementia.

He was transported from the hospital to a nursing facility. After a few months it became clear Mike was not going anywhere. This would be where he would finish his days. His dementia was increasing. He was on a pureed diet and strapped to either a wheelchair or a bed. I hated to see him that way.

Jo, whom I introduced in chapters 2 and 13, resigned herself to the new reality. Things had already been going downhill for Mike before this. He was losing his mobility and balance. His obsessive-compulsive disorder was intensifying. He was struggling to care for himself. His needs had become more than Jo could meet on her own. In a way, Mike's move into the nursing facility was a blessing for her.

After he had been there almost two years, Jo told me she wanted me to pray that Mike would experience a full recovery. Now, I have witnessed miracles. Jo, in fact, had been healed of cancer the year before. It was incredible. She had had a double mastectomy and twenty-four malignant nodes removed. Twenty-four! She remains cancer free. But this healing for Mike was something different. Or maybe not.

At any rate, I had a hard time wrapping my faith around it. Jo was insistent, though. She kept on asking me to pray every chance she could. I prayed, but I honestly did not have any expectations of recovery. Every time I visited Mike it seemed impossible—until last

Christmas.

We had been praying for recovery for about two months when I walked into the common area of the nursing facility, where about thirty residents were being entertained by a singer and a karaoke machine. I found the music painful, but most of the people seemed to be enjoying it. Mike obviously was. He was sitting in his wheelchair with his legs crossed and keeping the beat. This was different. I was used to finding him with his head sunk into his chest and his feet resting helplessly on the ground. You could not even push his chair without his feet dragging under it.

I sat down beside him, and he turned and said, "Hey, Paul. I sure am glad to see you!" He knew what day it was and asked about the church. He hoped to be there that coming Sunday. And he was. We went on to have the most normal conversation I have ever had with him, even before the dementia set in. His mind was as clear as a bell.

Before I left, I found his nurse and asked her what was going on with Mike. She said with bemusement, "We have no idea. It just happened all of a sudden. I've never seen anything like it."

☜ ☞

Mike started coming to church regularly in his wheelchair. He told me he wanted to walk again. Most nursing facilities do not want their folks walking around. It is too high of a fall risk. I wondered if they would even let him do this. I advised him, "Mike, there is absolutely nothing wrong with your legs except that you haven't used them in two years. Start doing the physical therapy." Then we prayed he would walk.

About five months later Jo called and asked if I could attend the next family consultation to talk about Mike's condition and progress. We sat around a table with the staff who were involved with caring for Mike. They wheeled him in and moved him to a regular chair, and the woman in charge of the meeting said, "Mr. Mike, say goodbye to your chair. You won't need that anymore." He looked as surprised as Jo and I. The woman went on to announce, "Today we are going to write up the plans for Mr. Mike's discharge. He's going home."

Jo, in her joy, began singing, "To God be the glory, great things he hath done!" She sang the entire first verse of that hymn and might have launched into the second had the administrator not gracefully continued with the meeting. I asked her how all this came to be, and she said, "It's what you think it is. We have no other explanation. It's a miracle."

At the end of the meeting they brought out a walker for Mike to use. He stood up like a man of forty years instead of his real age, seventy-one. I actually have it on video. He had no balance issues and looked strong on his feet. He took hold of the walker, and Jo and I followed him to his room. We could barely keep up with him. His problems with mobility, dementia, and diet, which had made it so difficult for Jo to care for him at home two years before, had completely vanished. One week later he went home.

When he walked into church the next Sunday, people were blown away. It was like the first Easter. I realize you would have to see it to believe it. I did.

What God did for Mike's mind, he did for my faith.

God gives life where there is none and family where there is none. Jo and Mike will always be part of my family because of the experiences and amazing blessings we have shared over the years.

Jim says . . .

Fred and Emily were two of my favorite people during my college years.

When I first knew them they were single. But love has its ways, and so it happened to Fred and Emily. They married, had children, and lived lives that contributed well to this world.

One day Emily discovered she had cancer. She did not get better.

Fred and Emily were people of deep faith.

After she died, Fred gathered their friends, and they prayed for Emily to come back to life.

Could it not happen? Did it not happen to Lazarus? Then why not to Emily? They prayed and prayed.

But Emily did not return to life in this world.

One day in my early years as a pastor I stood with Robert and Barbara. They looked into each other's eyes and took solemn vows to care for each other.

A few weeks before, when they approached me and asked if I would preside at their wedding, they told me a very surprising thing. They had been married before to each other, but the marriage had collapsed. They had divorced. The marriage was dead. Gone.

I agreed to meet with them for premarital counseling. We met on three occasions. We talked about the past and the future. We prayed.

Then one beautiful afternoon we gathered at their home with family and friends. Their son, Jared, a classmate of our twin sons, was there.

It was an afternoon of joy.

It was a day of resurrection!

༄ ༅

Maybe it is possible for dead people to come back to life. We believe there will be a day when God will raise up each and every one of God's people. But I have never seen this happen in this life.

I have, however, seen many other kinds of resurrections over the years.

> I have seen prodigal children come home.
>
> I have seen troubled marriages gain traction and husbands and wives blessed as they build a new relationship.
>
> I have seen people whose marriages have ended in divorce go on to find resurrection, new life, in a new relationship.
>
>> My sister Patricia is one of those people. Her marriage ended after thirty years. Followed by years that included joy in her family and friends but also a measure of loneliness.
>>
>> But then—resurrection. She met a man who, years later, still adores her. Cherishes her. And celebrates the grace of God that led them to become husband and wife.

The secret to resurrection is blessing encounters, brought about as we choose to bless one another.

Questions

1. What unbelievable things have you witnessed in your family?

2. How have those events affected your relationships with others and with God?

3. What is an area of your life in which you would like to see new life?

Family Challenge

Pray for the impossible with those people to whom God has attached you.

Prayer

O God of Resurrection power, pour faith into my heart, mind, and body that I may believe enough to ask for the impossible. Let me see your power at work in and through others, as well as in my own life. By faith I pray. Amen.

Epilogue

Jim says . . .

A good and faithful servant died last week.

Ed Cooley had been the pastor of two small churches in western Oklahoma for the past five years.

The sanctuary was standing room only as a bagpiper began the service. Two ministers spoke. David, a man who had come from Ithaca, New York, told us how Ed had been a great mentor in his life. A men's choir gave a remarkable rendering of the old hymn "Be Thou My Vision."

Ed and his wife, Loralee, had been married for almost forty-seven years.

After several years of marriage they had no children.

But then they became involved in a foster program, and a great saga began.

First was Jenni. Then Gail. Then Bridgette and Shaun. And Carla.

Eventually came Ed and Loralee's involvement with The Experiment in International Living, which led them to welcome Lizabeth and Angela, both from Brazil, into their home.

Over the years they also opened their hearts to Adriana and Thadria and Diana.

They had no children we would customarily refer to as "their own," but several rows of pews in the sanctuary held those who had become their children, their family.

The man from Ithaca told us that Ed had become like a father to him as his relationship with his future wife, Diana, developed.

When David proposed to Diana, he knew he would have to pass the Ed test.

At the time, David was not very involved in church, so he did not know how Ed would react to the news of Diana's engagement to him.

David learned, however, that Ed was a man who met people where they are.

No mention was made concerning David's lack of relationship with a church. Ed welcomed him into the fold, knowing that God would work on David in God's time and in God's way through the love of God's people.

Like many others, David knew Ed and Loralee were both second-mile people. They flew to New York to baptize David and Diana's first child.

Someone died, someone getting married—Ed and Loralee could be counted on to show up. That was how they were.

This is what blessing encounters are all about. They are about showing up.

They are about going the second mile.

They are about meeting people, without judgment, where they are.

Blessing encounters are about opening our lives to others in such a way that we are creating family.

One blessing at a time.

Paul says . . .

It is always a risk to engage with the people we encounter. We never really know what we are getting into when we do. I hope you will take the risk of moving toward people—and toward God. There is potential for family in every encounter if you are open to it. The greatest joys of life are the ones that are shared, and the greatest sorrow of life is to suffer alone. We were never meant to be alone.

There is a family awaiting you. It is bigger than you can imagine. You have much to give to it and much to receive from it. Your identity will be tied up in this family, and being part of it will make you more fully you. Yes, there will be headaches and heartaches. That is the cost of caring and sharing. But God has something to say about this.

God says . . .

Do not fear, for I have redeemed you;
    I have called you by name, you are
        mine.
When you pass through the waters, I
        will be with you;
    and through the rivers, they shall
        not overwhelm you;
when you walk through fire you shall
        not be burned,
    and the flame shall not
        consume you.
For I am the LORD your God,
    the Holy One of Israel, your Savior. . . .

you are precious in my sight,
  and honored, and I love you. . . .
Do not fear, for I am with you;
  I will bring your offspring from the
      east,
  and from the west I will gather you;
I will say to the north, "Give them up,"
  and to the south, "Do not withhold;
bring my sons from far away
  and my daughters from the end of
      the earth—
everyone who is called by my name,
  whom I created for my glory,
  whom I formed and made."

— Isaiah 43:1–3, 4, 5–7

Benediction

One day the angels sang as you entered the world.
You, a new blessing, had been welcomed to our planet.
Go and welcome others into your life.
Listen, help, open your heart, love.
Create blessing encounters wherever you go.
And when your last day arrives
you will go out with a heart filled with the
grace of our Lord Jesus Christ,
the love of God,
and the fellowship of the Holy Spirit.
Amen.

Notes

―

Preface
"Morning by morning" *The United Methodist Hymnal: Book of United Methodist Worship* (Nashville: United Methodist Publishing House, 1989), 140.

Chapter 1, Family
"When everything goes to hell" "Jim Butcher>Quotes>Quotable Quotes," *Goodreads*, accessed August 12, 2014, www.goodreads.com/quotes/66608-when-everything-goes-to-hell-the-people-who-stand-by/.

"under one head" and "seventeenth century" "Family," *Merriam-Webster*, accessed September 13, 2014, www.merriam-webster.com/dictionary/family/.

Chapter 3, Blessing
"a blessing from G-d" Brian Tice, "Day 5: The Biblical Meaning of 'Blessing,'" *Faith in Yeshua: Without Discrimination* (blog), *Adiakrisis*, accessed August 18, 2014, http://adiakrisis.wordpress.com/biblical-studies-articles/hebraic-observations-on-the-creation-narrative-genesis-11-23/day-5-the-biblical-meaning-of-blessing/.

Chapter 5, Strife
"is for the friction" M. Scott Peck, *A World Waiting to Be Born: Civility Rediscovered* ([N.Y.]: Random House, 2009), 105.

"The strife is o'er" *The United Methodist Hymnal: Book of United Methodist Worship* (Nashville: United Methodist Publishing House, 1989), 306.

Chapter 7, Jesus
"to love another person" "Victor Hugo>Quotes>Quotable Quotes," *Goodreads*, accessed August 12, 2014, www.goodreads.com/quotes/49720-to-love-another-person-is-to-see-the-face-of/.

Chapter 9, Siri
"beautiful woman" "How Did Siri Get Its Name?" *Forbes* (December 21, 2012), http://www.forbes.com/sites/quora/2012/12/21/how-did-siri-get-its-name/.

Chapter 11, Love
"make holy" "Bless," *Dictionary.com*, accessed October 4, 2014, http://dictionary.reference.com/browse/bless.

"kneel down" Jeff A. Benner, "Ancient Hebrew Word Meaning: Bless ~ barak," *Ancient Hebrew Research Center: Plowing through History, Aleph to Tav*, accessed October 4, 2014, http://www.ancient-hebrew.org/27_bless.html.

"make happy" "Bless," *Dictionary.com*.

Chapter 12, Welcoming
"Oh, Lord" CBS Interactive, "Oh, Lord, it's hard to be humble," *MetroLyrics*, accessed October 6, 2014, http://www.metrolyrics.com/its-hard-to-be-humble-lyrics-mac-davis.html.

Chapter 13, Church
"The word *educate*" "Educe," *Merriam-Webster*, accessed October 6, 2014, http://www.merriam-webster.com/dictionary/educe.

Chapter 18, Resurrection
"To God be the glory" *The United Methodist Hymnal: Book of United Methodist Worship* (Nashville: United Methodist Publishing House, 1989), 98.

Acknowledgements

—

Jim thanks . . .

By the grace of God I have been surrounded by blessing since the day I was born. My thanks go to all who have blessed me and taught me how to create family.

Special thanks go to my son Paul, who one day said, "Dad, I want you to write a book with me." This two-year-long project has been one of the great blessing encounters of my life.

Special thanks also to Elizabeth Lindsey, our editor. I have been astonished by the thoroughness of what has been an amazing labor of love. No editor could have nudged me along with the diplomatic toughness that has helped me say much more clearly what was on my heart and mind.

God has blessed me incredibly with the gift of my wife, Judy. During almost forty-five years of marriage I have watched her create family wherever she goes, blessing her family, friends, and the two thousand and more eighth-grade students she taught over the course of two decades. Her laughter, her quick smile, her calming touch, her innate goodness are at the heart of what led me to join our son in writing this book.

Thanks also to:

Paul's wife, Jennifer; our other children, David and John, and their wives, Jennifer and Kody; and our grandchildren, Allison, Christopher, Jude, Kieran, and Nelson. They have each blessed me in their own unique way.

My parents, Jim and Tense, who fed me, showed me right from wrong, and taught me loyalty to one's family

My sister, Patricia, who has been as good a friend as a brother could hope to have

My Burns and McGregor grandparents, who loved me as if I were great treasure

My aunts and uncles and cousins, who made family gatherings rich and special

My in-law family, including the dearest mother-in-law in the world, a father-in-law who always shot straight with me, and my wife's siblings, Melinda, Mark, and Nancy, and their families

A minister known simply as Mr. Adams, who helped me begin to love all my neighbors

A grade-school classmate named Terry, with whom best friendship and vast dreams were shared

Professor McIntyre, who taught me that physics was fun, although I always felt more blessed by his wisdom and gentle kindness than by the physics he taught

The Reverend Harold Wells, who preached sermons that first drew me closer to the Presbyterian church

The Reverend Jack Bennett, who baptized our twin sons and pointed me toward seminary

Stephen Atkinson, who opened my eyes to a life of Bible study, prayer, and the power of a small group of Christians who opened their lives to one another

Bill Priebe, best man in my wedding, who is different from me theologically and politically but graces me with the blessing that shows lion and lamb can lie down together

Seminary professor Dr. Robert Shelton, who took me deep and helped prepare me for the life of a pastor through his reminders to have a measure of humility, often grinning and saying such things as, "Remember, the Baptists may be right!"

The people of First Presbyterian Church in Lonoke, Arkansas, and Memorial Presbyterian Church in Norman, Oklahoma, who blessed me with their love, creativity, good humor, and willingness to follow me down what sometimes were wild-goose chases

My many, many colleagues in ministry, who have awed me by their skills and compassion and nourished me with their words and listening hearts

Paul thanks . . .

I would like to acknowledge the many people who played a part in the creation of this book.

First I would like to thank my father for his willingness to undergo the arduous task of writing a book with me. Sharing this work with him has been one of the greatest blessings of my life.

I want to thank my wife, Jennifer, for her ongoing support and patience in my various pursuits and passions.

A special thanks to the members of Priest Lake Presbyterian Church for giving me the opportunity to witness God's work firsthand in their loving worship, fellowship, and mission.

Further thanks to our editor, Elizabeth Lindsey, for her countless hours of work and her dedication to helping make this book as good as it could be.

And finally, I would like to give thanks for the person who inspired this book: Josephine Crenshaw. I saw in her a constant desire to bless others and a persistent pursuit to create the family she always wanted. Jo traveled to her heart's true home earlier this year.

About the Authors

James M. Burns, Jr.

James (Jim) Burns is a retired Presbyterian minister who served as the pastor of two churches. He received his PhD in physics from Texas A&M University and taught college physics for four years before his life direction changed and led him to Austin Presbyterian Theological Seminary and thirty-two years in the ministry.

He and his wife, Judy, live in Norman, Oklahoma, where he enjoys blessing encounters with his three sons and their wives, along with his five brilliant grandchildren.

Paul M. Burns

Paul Burns serves as the pastor of Priest Lake Presbyterian Church in Nashville, Tennessee. He holds an MDiv from Austin Presbyterian Theological Seminary. Prior to entering seminary, he worked as an investment consultant in New York City.

He lives in Hermitage, Tennessee, with his wife, Jennifer, his son, Nelson, and his dog, Chuy. He is the author of *Prayer Encounter: Changing the World One Prayer at a Time* and *Wider, Longer, Higher, Deeper: Forty Days of Prayer, Scripture, and Growth-filled Questions*.